NEW WRITING / BOOK TALK / NEWS AND REVIEWS

THE READER

No. 47 AUTUMN 2012

Published by The Reader Organisation

the reader
organisation

EDITOR   Philip Davis

DEPUTY EDITOR   Sarah Coley
CO-EDITORS   Maura Kennedy
                                Angela Macmillan
                                Eleanor McCann
                                Brian Nellist

ADDRESS   The Reader Magazine
                                The Reader Organisation
                                The Friary Centre
                                Bute Street
                                Liverpool
                                L5 3LA

EMAIL   magazine@thereader.org.uk
WEBSITE   www.thereader.org.uk
BLOG   www.thereaderonline.co.uk

DISTRIBUTION   See p. 127

COVER IMAGE   'Storm' by Pamela Sullivan;
                                ink on Fabriano paper

ISBN 978-0-9567862-6-5

SUBMISSIONS

The Reader genuinely welcomes submissions of poetry, fiction, essays, readings and thought. We publish professional writers and absolute beginners. Send your manuscript with SAE please to:

The Reader Organisation, The Friary Centre, Bute Street, Liverpool, L5 3LA

Printed and bound in the European Union by Bell and Bain Ltd, Glasgow

NEWS AUTUMN 2012

10TH GET INTO READING ANNIVERSARY

It began with one group of young mothers in St James' Library, Birkenhead, September 2002. Today we deliver 300+ weekly read aloud reading groups across the UK, with sister projects in Denmark and Australia; in hospitals, care homes, prisons, GP surgeries, libraries, supermarkets, homeless shelters, corporate board rooms, probation centres, schools and mental health day centres. Read **Jane Davis** on the last ten years on p.83.

MINTED: PRACTICAL POETRY FOR LIFE

Brian Nellist, the godfather of The Reader Organisation and *The Reader* magazine, has selected work from fifty poets that provide what he calls 'inexhaustible riches'. This anthology brings together poems written 1500–1900 which still resonate today: 'A travel brochure to encourage your own exploration'. See p.57.

RISE: READING IN SECURE ENVIRONMENTS

The **RISE** (Reading in Secure Environments) pilot project, will bring contemporary writers to Get Into Reading groups in secure criminal justice and mental health care settings. Funded by Arts Council England, we are in partnership with five literature festivals across the U.K. The first RISE author events are in October with **Jackie Kay**, **Joe Dunthorne**, **Inua Ellams** at the Manchester Literature Festival and **Michael Stewart** and **Jean Sprackland** at the Durham Book Festival.

NEW COMMISSIONS

The Historic Royal Palaces charity has commissioned a Get Into Reading group at Kensington Palace. A part-time reader-in-residence has been appointed in Southwark. Devon Libraries have funded new groups across the county, while Tesco have renewed funding for a second year of work with their Community Champions programme.

Buy *Minted* from The Reader Organisation to support our work and find out more about all of our activities on **www.thereader. org.uk**

CONTENTS

THREE PEAKS CHALLENGE

Fourteen hardy fundraisers scaled Britain's 3 highest peaks and raised over £9,000 for The Reader Organisation's care leavers' Apprenticeship Fund.

EDITORIAL

THE SCORE: OPUS 64

GET INTO READING 10TH ANNIVERSARY

Philip Davis

I t was an amateur performance of Mendelssohn's violin concerto many years ago in Cambridge. I loved Mendelssohn but did not have a clue why. Perhaps it had something to do with a sorrow in the music that had within it both its own power and the power to fight against itself. At any rate, I remember as a youth regularly looking at a cheap framed picture of him in the local junkshop and thought of buying it day after day. But I never did, and if I had I probably would not have taken so much notice of it as I do now in my memory, though I still regret not buying it.

But of this performance: I don't remember whether it was the end of the first movement or, more likely, the finale of the third and last one, but the thing was going at a furious pace. It *had* to go, like a plane nearing the velocity of take-off, irresistible and unstoppable.

To one side of the violin soloist, who was leading the race, there was the first cellist, an intense young woman. As the pace was forced on and on, and the music rose and rose, and the soloist asked more and more again of all those around him, the cellist, bowing furiously, had to move the fingers of her other hand ever faster and ever higher up the frets. And right at the last, at the very top, I saw her hand slip and miss it.

The orchestra just went on triumphantly without her, and the music flew by, leaving her behind like some stranded little island after a great rush of waters. She looked suddenly like a defeated person, winded and isolated.

I was an ignorant spectator, without musical education. And though I felt very sorry for her in her public pain, what I was really thinking was only how great it would have been had she actually made it, that final top push. Even then I realised that if she had made it, paradoxically I would not have known quite how great an effort it took. That's why I sometimes think this failure was the greatest musical experience I have witnessed. I saw the moment when the musician and the person separated in the midst of a performance. It was like an imaginative reversal of the magic by which the one became the other in the step-up of achieved art.

I often recall a moment in Stanley Middleton's *An After-Dinner's Sleep* in which it is reported that a barrister and his wife always go to Christmas Midnight Mass at their local church. 'I don't know why we bother,' says the husband, 'we don't get on with the vicar, the choir's hopeless, and the organist's got a wooden leg.' Why don't you go to a better place with good music, asks a visitor:

> **'You're right. That's what we ought to do.'**
> **'Why don't we?' Susan asked.**
> **'I wonder if it's because seeing something happen at its most humdrum gives you a better insight into its nature.'**

I used to work for a little time in a department of music in the university, in an administrative role, and loved hearing the students practise in some room above me whilst I was doing a mundane task at the computer. The rough rehearsals often seemed more valuable to me than the apparently smooth performances. Middleton himself used to play double-bass in our school orchestra, happy to be the backing-up. But there is an aftermath to that story of the Mendelssohn performance. About six months later the cellist was involved in a minor car-accident which put her into hospital, scarred and under careful cranial observation for some time. By some sort of happenstance which I know a reader will think highly unlikely, I had been telling a friend about the Mendelssohn concert and she not only knew the cellist but knew of her recent accident and was going to visit her that day in the local hospital. As if it were a sign (from God know's where), I asked whether I could go along and I did so. Not that my naïvete ended there. When I actually told the stricken cellist how moved I had been by the performance, including most of all her miss, she said to me, quite evenly, 'Do you know anything about music?'

So I stick to my literary guns. When Thomas Hardy was aged 22 and new in London, he would go to concerts and operas, loyally supporting an English Opera Company. There, it is said in *The Life of Thomas Hardy* ghosted by his second wife, 'he had the painful experience of hearing the gradual breakdown of the once fine voice of William Harrison':

Hardy was heard to assert that, as it were in defiance of fate, Harrison would sing night after night his favourite songs, such as 'Let me like a soldier fall' in *Maritana* [by William Vincent Wallace], and, particularly, 'When other lips' in *The Bohemian Girl* [by Michael William Balfe], wherein his complete failure towards the last attempts would move a sensitive listener to tears : he thought Harrison's courage in struggling on, hoping against hope, might probably cause him to be remembered longer than his greatest success.

This was the hope of the pessimist, with all those forgotten names, Wallace, Balfe, Harrison.

But to finish my story. Years later, in the music department in Liverpool and still knowing little, I admired the way the students committed themselves to their instrumental playing, though the course was primarily academic rather than performative. It wasn't a conservatoire, and none of them was going to go on to become a professional member of an orchestra, let alone a soloist. But there was something powerful in their willing apprenticeship. What is the point of trying, what good is it, asks vain young Gwendolen in George Eliot's *Daniel Deronda*, if I can never be a great singer? The answer given is that the effort means still belonging to something great, knowing something great, even if one cannot oneself be great at it.

So with these students-apprentices, *doing* the music was part of learning music, and it played back into their academic studies. I kept thinking: when I get back to my own department, the department of literature, is there anything equivalent that for my students would be the *doing* of literature?

I didn't think of a creative writing course or a module in drama-in-performance. I thought instead about reading aloud and the doing of reading aloud in outreach work, outside the university in schools amongst children not interested in books. It was the work The Reader Organisation was already doing with its Get Into Reading programme.

As you will read elsewhere in this issue, Get Into Reading is ten years old this September. I have seen undergraduates reporting on their experience of reading aloud one-to one with children in need or care or trouble. It is not only what these students have given these children that is luminous but what the experience has given the students. When they speak of it, they know something real – something raw, difficult, full of stammerings and difficulties, but idealistic and possible, like Mendelssohn's violin pushing the players to the final notes of a strong yearning.

EDITOR'S PICKS

Janet Suzman writes a fierce and funny defence of Shakespeare's right to be known as the writer of his own plays. In new fiction we have young and old. **John Kinsella**'s 'Africa Reef' is a tale of growing up that focuses on a boy's experience at sea; **Christine Shaw**'s 'The Glazed Maquette' tells of a retired woman who copes with her grumpy family and who finds life (as glimpsed through her neighbour's windows) enthralling.

Rebecca Goss writes movingly on her poem 'Her Birth' for Poet on Her Work. New poetry from **Alison Brackenbury, John Levett, Charles Wilkinson, Pat Farrington** and the recent Poet Laureate for Birmingham, **Roy McFarlane**.

September sees the tenth anniversary of The Reader Organisation's read aloud programme, Get Into Reading, an occasion marked here by Jane Davis's retrospective and her interview with **Joseph Gold**, a pioneer in the field of reading personally. In the first of a new series, **Grace Farrington** gives preliminary research reports on reading groups.

Our publishing empire expands! **Angela Macmillan** of 'Buck's Quiz' and 'Books About...' has a new book in time for Christmas, *A Little, Aloud for Children* (David Fickling Books, £9.99). Visit our website to get it for a mere £5.99 + p&p. **Brian Nellist**, guiding force for the magazine, launches his poetry anthology *Minted* on 27 September. Read his latest 'Ask the Reader' on p.93.

FREE CHRISTMAS GIFT SUBSCRIPTION

If you subscribe to the *The Reader** we would like to offer you a free gift subscription for a person of your choosing. Visit **www.thereader.org.uk** or email **magazine@thereader.org.uk** for further details. Orders for gift subscriptions must be received by 23 November to ensure Christmas delivery within the UK.

*and have not already given a gift subscription

Subscription information, p.128

FACE TO FACE

MEET THE POET

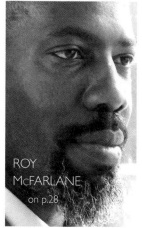

ROY
McFARLANE
on p.28

Which poet would you like to have met?
It would have to be Langston Hughes, just
to be able to go back in time and walk the
streets of Harlem, get caught up in the Harlem
Renaissance during a period where the fabric
of society was being stretched and pulled by
the issues of racism and poverty. Langston
stood tall in this period and managed to
capture the voices of the marginalised, evoke
the struggle of everyday people with poetry
that was profound but yet lyrical and musical.

'What is poetry?'
 Intensity.
Much in a little.

ALISON
BRACKENBURY
on p.40

What poems do you carry in your mind and why?
Fulke Greville's 'Chorus Sacerdotum' for its metrical concision, wisdom and resignation – a resignation that turns, by the end of the poem, into Elizabethan affirmation. At the other end of the spectrum Wallace Steven's 'Tea At The Palaz Of Hoon'. Enigmatic and puzzling, its beauty lodges in the mind long before you try to tease out any sense. There are many poems in between but these exemplify the extremes of driven meaning and loosely floating beauty; balancing the tension between the two seems to me to be one of the ways in which poetry works.

JOHN
LEVETT
on p.62

CHARLES
WILKINSON
on p.8

Which poet would you like to have met?
A poet to share a glass or two? No, an evening with a resurrected Dylan Thomas would be hazardous to health and pocket. Now I'm over sixty, it's politic to opt for a medical man. Scottish-born Gael Turnbull, who like William Carlos Williams, another poet-doctor, received his training at the University of Pennsylvania, was an excellent writer in the modernist manner. As a publisher, he did much to bring American poets, such as Robert Creeley, to a British public. I don't share his predilection for morris-dancing, but he'd have had much to tell me about poetry and publishing on both sides of the Atlantic.

Which poet would you like to have met?
I would like to have met John Clare (1793-1864), the first modern Nature poet. As his publisher said, he 'looked on Nature's face as if she were a living friend he might lose', which resonates with contemporary threats to the natural world. I love the idea that he often wrote sitting in a field with 'his hat serving for his desk'. This explains some of the immediacy of his work; it's as if you can see everything from inside his head. I deepened my appreciation of Clare writing about him in an article for *Orbis*, called 'From Paradise to Apocalypse? Some historical contrasts in Nature poetry'.

PAT
FARRINGTON
on p.96

REBECCA GOSS
© Rosie Bennett

THE POET ON HER WORK

ON 'HER BIRTH'

Rebecca Goss

Her Birth

On the wall, a print of purple petunias,
watercoloured in Walberswick.
I call to you, say *That's a good omen*,

that's a good sign, before buckling,
gripping the hospital bed.
Walberswick is where I holidayed,

every childhood summer.
It's where we announced *the news*.
Sixteen months after the effort

of her birth, we collect a faux-walnut
box from Jenkins & Sons. Inside,
a clear sachet, weightless as dried herbs.

We drive 281 miles for that cold, unstoppable
wave to suck the sachet clean and I ask you,
She is alright now, isn't she? She is alright?

First published at www.shadowtrain.com

On the 21st of March 2007, I gave birth to my first child, Ella. Delivered in eight hard, but straightforward hours at Liverpool Women's Hospital, we celebrated her arrival for a day. Whilst packing up my hospital bag and getting ready to take her home, a paediatrician came to check Ella was well enough to leave the hospital – a standard procedure. After a few minutes, the doctor told me she thought Ella was looking a little blue and together we took my baby to the neo-natal intensive care unit 'for a bit of oxygen'. Within the hour, Ella was diagnosed with Severe Ebstein's Anomaly – a rare heart condition for which there is no cure.

This poem is taken from a book length sequence I am writing about Ella's life and death. It begins in the hospital room in which I gave birth to her. As a pregnant woman, I shunned all baby books and 'How To' manuals. I rejected the idea of there being a 'right way' to have a baby. I wanted to trust my instincts. I did however find myself thinking about good omens and signs. Meeting my midwife for the first time soon revealed she had lived in my house, over twenty years ago, as a lodger. She was excited to be back in a house she once loved and I thought it could only be a good omen that she knew my home. I was very sick for the first three months of my pregnancy. Older, wiser mothers will tell you, sickness is often taken as a sign that things are progressing well.

The biggest sign of all came when I walked into the hospital room where I would give birth to Ella. A large Charles Rennie Mackintosh print of purple petunias hung above the bed. With my labour advancing and my body restless, I moved around the room, stopping to peer at the picture and breathe hard against its glass. There, beneath slim stems, I saw the word Walberswick, written in the artist's hand. Walberswick is a tiny village on the Suffolk coast and a formative place in my childhood, as the poem explains. I beckoned to my husband and tapped on the glass. It was going to be alright. It was all going to be good.

My poems are characteristically short. 'Her Birth' was written a few months after Ella died and early drafts are much more detailed. In them I identify Mackintosh, I describe the flowers, I tell of champagne shared with my family in The Bell (Walberswick's best pub), I include a midwife's presence, I describe my husband's trousers rolled to his shins as he enters the water. All of that was cut. It went from twenty-four lines to fifteen in ten drafts. I wanted to concentrate on the actions: my body 'buckling' in labour, the ashes being collected, the driving, the scattering, the unstoppable waves. I wanted to propel the poem forward from that place of anticipation and excitement to the revelation that we only had Ella for a short time.

I have spent hours thinking about how I got my 'signs' so wrong and I wanted an undercurrent of disbelief to run through the poem. For me, that's where the word 'effort' comes in. Firstly there was the effort of pregnancy and birth. During our first night in intensive care, still confounded by what had happened to Ella, I remember whispering to my husband, 'But I worked so hard to look after her'. I could not accept that despite all the effort to bring Ella into the world, we were going to lose her. There were Ella's daily efforts to breathe and grow. All the effort made to keep her alive and make her sixteen months of life (much longer than predicted) as normal as possible. The effort it took my husband to walk into the sea with that pocket of ash and the effort it's taken consequently, for us to carry on without her.

I had to think long and hard about how to describe Ella's ashes. I didn't want the poem to be littered with funereal language. I didn't want to use the words ashes, undertaker or urn. They felt too heavy for this poem and too adult; they felt associated with adult deaths. This is about a child so the language had to be different. The idea of herbs came after thinking about the slight contents of the sachet. I wanted to describe her mass becoming almost nothing at all. Something so small you could hold it in one hand.

The last line of the poem is exactly as I said it. Up until that point, Ella had been so far away from me since she'd died. As a tiny baby and a poorly small child who never crawled or walked, she quite literally never left my arms, but after her death she was kept in a hospital morgue, an undertaker's, a 'faux-walnut box'. Yet I saw her as still existing in some way. For that long drive to Suffolk, I had her back with me, until she touched the sea. It was only then I began to understand she was gone.

I believe grief must be articulated in order to survive it. A child's death is incredibly difficult territory to navigate but I strive to make my poems about Ella accessible. Of course the subject matter is extremely sad, but I hope the poems are not sentimental in any way. Rather, I intend them to be honest and moving. I want to prove with this collection that you can write and talk about something very distressing, but you don't have to frighten or alienate your audience.

I've done a lot of public speaking about Ella. I've read the poems at literary festivals and universities, but in 2009 I was invited to read at the Child Bereavement Charity's annual conference for NHS staff. The purpose of the conference was to discuss the impact of losing a baby. The charity uses a variety of speakers to illustrate to NHS staff that every family's experience is profoundly different. They had not had a poet speak at a conference before. I read to an audience of paediatric consultants, nurses, midwives, health visitors, counsellors, hospital chaplains, bereaved parents and undertakers, some of whom had never had a poem read to them in their lives. I was particularly moved by the feedback I received afterwards. People came to tell me they had experienced things in my poems, but had been unable to explain them in detail. That's what I want to do with this collection - draw the reader in to look very closely at the details of dying and bereavement. I read 'Her Birth' at the conference. I didn't find the poem particularly easy to read aloud, but I'm glad I've written it. The moment has been explained, expressed and shared. It's been done succinctly and yes, there is an element of it being 'dealt with'. Sometimes, the exhausting replaying of a scene in my mind will cease, once I have written a poem about it.

In 2010, I had another baby, again born at the Women's Hospital in Liverpool. Late one July night, baby most definitely on its way, my husband and I walked into an exact replica of the room I'd given birth to Ella in. Same layout, same colour on the walls, same print. I sat on the bed and sobbed. A midwife came to sit beside me, wrapped an arm around my shoulders and asked if I was crying because of the pain. I remember how I almost scoffed at her. How could anything hurt me as much as losing Ella? Once she knew about the Mackintosh print and its upsetting history, the midwife was terrific. She walked straight up to it and to our astonishment, slid the picture (frame and all) to one side. Behind it, like something out of a Bond film, were tubes, oxygen masks and much more medical paraphernalia. I suddenly realised we were staring at everything that was missing from this hospital room. It is policy at Liverpool Women's to hide it all. For many women, giving birth will include their first ever visit to a hospital. This can lead to high levels of anxiety, made worse when they see strange and frightening medical equipment, so it is disguised. I thought this was a brilliant idea and began to see the print as a clever, necessary part of what was about to happen. The midwife also told me that every room in the delivery wing looks exactly the same. I stopped believing in signs and concentrated on giving birth to a healthy little girl, who we named Molly.

I think the collection will be titled *Her Birth* but since having Molly, I have decided to finish it with a short sequence about the joys and complexities of having another child.

We took Molly to Walberswick when she was one. Parked up by the dunes, we pushed her pram towards the sea, lifted it over the final rise, dropped down onto pebbles and the deserted beach. For a time, we just stood there, facing the spray, before deciding the best way was to free Molly from straps and carry her in. My husband held her tight against his coat, his spare hand locked in mine. We waded forward, into that same cold pull and lifted Molly high above our heads. She squealed, laughing in the wind. We cried beneath her, as waves splashed inside our wellington boots. Back on the sand, I steered the pram but my husband carried Molly back to the car. She wriggled and resisted, as normal toddlers do, but I'm sure he was unwilling to give up her squirming, living limbs.

JOHN KINSELLA
© Tracy Ryan

FICTION

AFRICA REEF

John Kinsella

Dylan heard that it was called Africa Reef because it was 'halfway to Africa'. It was a long way out to sea, out in the open ocean, a weird protrusion surrounded by deep waters. Maybe an island that hadn't yet formed, or had been swallowed by the waves. He wasn't sure, and when he asked, he got no more than the apparent reason for its name, though more often than not it was said, 'halfway to bloody Africa'.

He did know, though, that this new town he was living in was on the 'shipwreck coast', where for hundreds of years ships had come to grief. And out at the Islands, there had been mutiny and mass murder. The local museum was full of relics from the early days of European exploration and the watery graves of fate. With apprehension and excitement, he pieced this together in his head, making a narrative that compelled him to accept his new best friend's offer to visit Africa Reef, Saturday afternoon on his father's boat.

At least it compelled him to ask his mum, who rang the other boy's father and talked it over. After ascertaining that the father was a police sergeant and all passengers on his boat would wear life-jackets, she gave a nervous, cautious 'okay'. Two other former best friends of the sergeant's son would be shipping out as well. The boat would be back at the marina by dark, and they'd all be home soon after that. The weather was still warm and soothing.

The boys were all thirteen. Dylan was excited to be living in a new place, but the other boys were keen to leave the coastal town and go just about anywhere else. Eighteen miles out to sea, straight out into the wide ocean, certainly qualified as 'anywhere else', and though they considered themselves too old and too sophisticated to say they were embarking on an 'adventure', they all secretly felt it to be the case.

Dylan had just started reading *The Old Man and the Sea* for English, with his usual lack of enthusiasm, but now he decided to get stuck into it, and the book he'd seen on his Gran's shelf, *The Cruel Sea*, though he knew nothing about that one and couldn't pronounce the author's name.

Dylan walked down to the beach every day after school and stared out long and hard, filling his head with the vastness. He had come from far inland where there was also vastness, but a vastness that was red and dry; or on those rare occasions when water came, it was a huge flood that vanished after a few days. But what the sea and the desert had in common was the immensity of the sky itself, arching over both like a protective dome, keeping things in and out, keeping and making secrets. The sky seemed to be the reason for the desert's existence, and the sea's existence.

The police sergeant, with his son and the two other boys, collected Dylan from outside his house on Saturday, after an early lunch. Dylan's mum had a quick, reassuring chat with the sergeant, and hugged her son, reminding him to be sensible and do what he was told. Normally Dylan would have been embarrassed, but he was too excited to care and the other boys were the same. One of them, Serge, whom Dylan knew least, did scowl and smile at the same time in a way that was ambiguous, but not ambiguous enough to spend any time thinking about.

And it was through the back window of the car, and Dylan's eyes were *really* on the twenty-foot boat that sat on the trailer behind the four-wheel drive. He'd seen it before, at his mate's place. It was called Hilda, after the sergeant's wife. It didn't seem that big really, but it did have a large outboard motor – an Evinrude – on the back.

The boys hopped out of the car once they reached the marina so the sergeant could back the boat-trailer down the ramp. His son directed him with precision, knowing his dad had little patience for showing off, especially when doing something serious. Once the trailer was submerged, the sergeant winched the boat down, down, down into the green water. Wading in up to his waist, he directed the boat around the ramp and, taking a rope hooked to the bow, dragged it to the small beach area alongside. There were other craft he had to avoid, but since he was a well-known local, the other weekend sailors did their best to avoid him.

He called to all the boys to hold the rope while he jumped in and got the sheet anchor, which he tossed into clear space on the shore, and jumped out to secure. The boys, champing to get onto the boat, held its bow while the sergeant parked the four-wheel drive and trailer exactly where they should be. Then the boys clambered on board. The sergeant retrieved the anchor and towed the boat out, then climbed aboard himself. He told his son to lower the outboard; then, just as the other boys thought they were drifting too close to the marina jetty, he started the engine and turned the boat out towards open sea. Dylan was overwhelmed as he sat with the others at the back — at the 'stern', watching the water churning and frothing, the propeller digging its furious, white wake.

As the boat skipped along past the grain ships moored outside the shipping lanes, Dylan considered the only way to confront, to absorb such vastness was in the orderly manner of the sergeant, who said nothing more than necessary. Occasionally one of the other boys hooted with joy, but the sergeant's son was clearly on duty with his father, watching for any sign of a command, and if he was enjoying himself it was only in a form specific to his relationship with his father. The two former best friends, who were very close, pointed to the town they were leaving behind, muttering under their breath and barely restraining their excitement. They didn't invite Dylan into their conversation, which they directed over the engine's roar and the hull's slap slap slap on the gentle swell. Dylan didn't mind this.

When Dylan noticed the waterspout on the horizon, he said nothing, because he didn't understand what it was. He was sure, though, that no one else had seen it, because he had trained his eye to see so far into the distance, into the vastness, that he hardly believed anyone else could see that far or in that way. But the others did notice clouds forming on the horizon, and the sergeant half-yelled above the boat-noise, Have to keep an eye on that, the weather comes up fast out here.

But he kept the boat going at a steady pace, and a half-hour passed before he spoke again.

That cloud's building and the wind is picking up, boys, so we might play it safe and head back in today. We can come out on another day. The two former best friends moaned a little, but the sergeant's son cut them a look that said, don't do it, my father's not in the mood.

Dylan wondered where the shore was. He considered the sun, which was fast vanishing behind thick cloud, and thought he'd worked it out. The boat was old, but had a compass and all the safety gear, and they all felt over-protected rugged up in their orange life-jackets. The sergeant cut back on the throttle and curved the boat around.

Look, boys! he called, dolphins.

His son, no longer able to restrain the excitement he'd been sitting on, burst out. Please, Dad, because we're going back and not getting to see Africa Reef, can we just sit here for a few minutes and watch the dolphins?

The sergeant looked at the boys, all well-behaved, and said, Just for a few minutes. The sky's getting dark out there and it's coming in. We don't want to get caught.

And the boat was rocking much more than it had been, and with the engine idling, it started to tilt in ways it hadn't tilted before. The dolphins surfaced, submerged, surfaced, submerged, appeared a long way off, then vanished.

Okay, boys, said the sergeant, we're off. He pushed the throttle lever out of idle position and accelerated. The engine sputtered and died. He tried to restart, and it sputtered and died again. Another death later, he said, gruffly, Move out of the way, boys, and went to check the fuel tank, and then the motor itself.

Enough fuel, he said, squeezing the bulb and checking the indicator. Motor doesn't smell flooded.

He messed with it a while, though he had trouble because the swell was gaining strength, tossing him and the boys together. Watch it, boys! he roared. Dylan retreated to the cabin area under the bow deck. The other boys followed him, except the sergeant's son who was stationed at the wheel, holding on as if all life depended on it. Dylan felt a jab in his back, and looked around to see Serge snarling at him, Out of my way, you dork, he said just loud enough for Dylan alone to hear. You're a bloody stranger, mate, and if anyone's getting the comfy position it's not going to be you.

Dylan moved, and looked out at the sergeant, the dead motor, the vast sky black in all directions now. A strong wind was cutting across the boat and spinning it like a top. Every time the boat went side-on to the swell, it felt as if it was going to tip and capsize. Dylan rolled onto Serge, who openly thumped him and yelled to the sergeant, This guy's a dag, Sir, he's rolling onto me like a girl. The sergeant yelled against the wind, Act like a man, son! Dylan knew the instruction was meant for him.

As the sergeant worked frantically at the motor, barking at his son to 'turn it over' now and again, he began to swear. Fucking ass of a thing, fucking bastard. The fucking battery will be flat next and then we'll be well and truly fucked. The swell was getting massive and there was fear in everyone's eyes, even the angry sergeant's.

Then, on his father's instructions, the son turned the ignition again, and the engine fired into life. The sergeant lurched to the wheel, pushed his son aside and said, Hold on, everyone! He faced the boat into the pitch of the waves, and started towards the shore, rubbing the top of the boat's compass as if it were a talisman. He called to his son to look for the flares in the front of the boat, and have them ready if need be.

Serge and the other boy were clinging to each other, then Serge vomited and vomited. Dylan noticed Serge had literally turned green, but he didn't find any satisfaction in this. He just stayed still and stared into the place where the sun should have been, where all life came from. He thought of the desert sun, the inland sun he'd grown up with. It could burn you alive in no time, but he missed it.

The sea had become the smallest place in existence: it wasn't vastness, just weight, crushing weight. It felt as if it was going to break through the hull at any time. Water was sloshing through the cabin. Soon, with the sergeant's son, he was working the bilge pump, unsure who told him to do so or how he knew what to do, or even what it was. Serge looked like death, and Dylan feared him. The other boy held Serge tight and Dylan thought it'd be nice to have a friend who cared so much. He'd had friends like that out in the desert and yet had been to eager to leave them. To go somewhere, anywhere. Africa. Africa Reef. His friends had been closing in on him. He'd felt he was losing the key to the vastness, the space.

They broke through the edge of the storm, and the sea began slowly to settle. The sergeant looked at Serge's vomit but not at Serge. To his son he said simply, You can clean up that mess when we get home. Should have done it over the bloody side. There was shame everywhere. Dylan thought of saying, I'll help, but knew that it was better to say nothing. He wasn't trying to win friends, and he wasn't trying to make enemies.

When they got back to shore and had managed to hoist the boat up on the trailer, Dylan wondered about Hilda, the sergeant's wife. He'd met her a few times and she was so beautiful and soft. He wondered how it would have all gone if she'd been on the boat, rather than just her name.

The sergeant spread plastic sheets over the seats of his car. He said to Serge, You should really walk home, but when Serge started off on trembling legs, covered in vomit and soaked to the skin, he called, I was joking! Before allowing the boys to get into the car, he said, Look out at the sea, boys. Never take it for granted.

And they did look. Dylan saw another water spout, but as

no one mentioned it, he assumed that he alone could see it, and kept his mouth firmly shut. A new town, a new way of life. He pondered how the water spout's grey-white reminded him of the dust devil's red-white swirl in the desert, spouts of dust joining desert and sky. And Dylan knew the sea and the sky had reasons for sharing or not sharing their secrets.

POETRY

ROY McFARLANE

I found my father's love letters

I found my father's love letters
in strange and obscure places,
hidden in dark secret spaces,
where memories had closed the doors.

I found blank letters, with matching cards and envelopes.
A small drawer filled with letters unfinished,
crossed through, curling at the edges,
turning in the colour of time.

There was one in Marquez's *Love in the Time of Cholera*
sandwiched somewhere between
Fermina's rejection of Floretina
and a lifetime of loving, waiting for true love.

I found some penned in a note pad, half-written, half-thought,
scribbled to capture fleeting thoughts,
earnest in writing the emotional overflow
that time edits into streams flowing over with love.

I found one folded
lost in the attic
an elegy to love
that time had forgotten.

I searched to find the true name to those letters entitled my love.
A secret lover? Distant lover? First time lover?
or even my mother of whom you gave a thousand names
but I never heard you call her *my love.*

I wonder if they ever received their letters,
an amended version, a completed version
refined and acceptable, filled with rose petals,
signed and sealed with your love.

Talking for both of us

Conversations turned to zero
during teenage days,
words far and few between us
mirroring the distance
and time we spent together.
From teenager to young man.
I thought I knew it all,
lost in love, my first love,
imagined I was all potent
but impotent in the words
I shared with my old man.
From young man to married man.
Got caught up in the labour and strife
of married life that drove me
to conversations over telephones
and sharing words
whilst passing through
for Sunday dinners.
From married man to fatherhood.
Now we're conversing as my
firstborn brings us together
to have conversations
full and overflowing
with laughter as we speak
with familiar tongues.
From father back to son again.
I'm speechless as I watch
the stroke bind your tongue
turning our conversations
into one way traffic.
I talk about everything and anything
to catch up with all the years
that my foolish youth had wasted.

And you bow your head
your tongue failing
to form the words
that drawls and dribbles
from your lips.
So I wipe the corners of your mouth
as I talk for both of us.
Finally.
        Old Father Time
takes you away and
I'm standing over you
giving an eulogy
and I stop talking
for a moment at the loss of you.

JOSEPH GOLD

INTERVIEW

A WORLD FOR OURSELVES

Jane Davis talks to Joseph Gold

Joseph Gold was born in London, attended the University of Birmingham and received his PhD from the University of Wisconsin. An instructor and professor for over 40 years, he is a clinical member of the American Association for Marriage and Family Therapy and author of books on Charles Dickens and William Faulkner, as well as the inspirational *Read for Your Life: Literature as a Life Support System* and *The Story Species: Our Life-Literature Connection*. His books explain how we can make use of fiction and poetry in constructing, repairing and understanding our own lives. He lives in Northern Ontario.

What do you remember about learning to read?

My earliest memories and associations were about reading connected to my mother, she loved to read, so my first great gift as a child was that I had a mother who loved to read. I have a vivid imagination and played parts with everything I read or saw. *Mother Goose* was a favourite and *Wind in the Willows* by Kenneth Grahame. *Wind in the Willows* has always been my favourite expression of what I love best about England and still is. In fact, I cannot ever remember being moved or comfortable in cities. I am not taken in by Wordsworth's love sonnet on London, ('Composed Upon Westminster Bridge') in which the city is seen as the country's 'mighty heart', but only when everyone is asleep, there is no traffic, no noise and no activity.

I fell in love with words, *sound*, language, how these sounds related to my life. It was part of an expanding world; I can't separate language from the world.

So were you a great talker as a little boy?

I was loquacious. I remember wanting to read the pages for myself. That was a hidden kind of magic, and I had that power. Many years later when I taught at The University of Waterloo, Ontario, after dinner on many evenings in the old farmhouse where I lived, my three children became part of a great focus on my reading at the table. They kept close account of whose turn it was to sit on my lap. Most vividly I remember reading Damon Runyon. I never could do a Brooklyn accent, but I certainly tried and my children loved it. They savoured it. I shared Dickens with them too. I have a great admiration for Dickens. He was always in a struggle between doing something socially and writing stories, and he sometimes tripped over that double goal to be both entertaining and serious.

Did you come to the American continent as a graduate student?

Yes, I came over, from Birmingham University to take out a teaching assistantship at Wisconsin and do my PhD. I was told by a physician there that I would not do well in the States! My health would be affected, he said, because I argued with so much social injustice; it's a very violent and hard place. He told me that Americans have a protection that they grow from being born there, and I didn't have it of course, so he could see me getting an ulcer or getting very sick.

Canada's quite different, or it used to be anyway. We have got a government now that wants to make it more like America. This hardening is continuous with what is going on in the academy. There is a war going on there with the people who don't want our reading to be affected by feelings, who expect books to be read according to critical rules. Universities are effectively screening out the students who want to read with feeling.

It used to be very different. The old idea was that everyone in American Universities, *every* student in *every* department would take an English course in literature, which is why they needed teaching assistants, there were so many students. But everyone had this injection of culture and shared knowledge. The students got a lot from it. Now the universities teach theory, which is a design to kill off any engagement with reading. But they have got a dilemma; they are losing students and they are panicking because they have got to keep the enterprise going. They are not going to get publicly funded if they are talking to each other in a sort of late-blooming scholastic sense.

What do you think should be done about it?

The first-year course that I would like to foster, would contain material that would convey some sense to students of their own neurology, an awareness of what is going on in them while they read. There is a very good book called *Reading in the Brain* by Stanislas Deheane. He explains how the reading process takes place neurologically. I would give the students this so that they would know reading is not a non-science; we just haven't got there yet.

I was looking this morning at your books on reading, Read for Your Life *and* The Story Species. *What you are describing in your course here is, in a way, an amalgam of both those books where you want students a) to know what's happening in the brain and b) to develop an emotional awareness of what's happening to* them *as they read.*

Yes, it's both things, a and b. There is the need for an accessible textbook for students of literature that gives at least some idea of the neural processes, that take place in language, both forming and receiving oral and written narrative. We have been discussing such a textbook.

Antonio Damasio is a celebrated American neuroscientist. He has been working hard to establish emotion as an essential part of the human thinking complex. In his most personal book, *Looking for Spinoza*, he goes to Holland in search of the spirit or essence of the seventeenth century philosopher. Damasio called an earlier book *Descartes' Error* (Descartes and Spinoza were contemporaries). Descartes left emotion out of his theory of mind.

INTERVIEW

Damasio says that this was a serious and long-prevailing error that has set back brain studies until recently. And even now the error persists and it certainly persists in education. There is fear of emotion. But only psychopaths can read or hear stories without experiencing emotion.

The great Colombian story writer, Gabriel Garcia Marquez, says he writes for his friends, his friends being those who can feel and apprehend the emotions that shape his work.

In a paper my wife wrote for a course, she experimented with letters that a friend might write to Marquez about his story, 'Balthazar's Marvelous Afternoon'. I could see this as a form of literary criticism based on the emotional and cognitive connection between the writer and reader.

That's interesting because often writers appear like friends when we are reading. They feel like that.

That is something that I would aim for in my students. I think they should be given the opportunity to understand how ideology is the archetypal opposite of experience, human experience. Ideology is characterised by its denial of experience and ideologues will keep doing what they do without regard to experience. It doesn't matter to them if it doesn't work; their ideology will tell them to keep doing it, in fact they will do *more* of it when it doesn't work.

So what would you include on your course, what books?

Nathaniel Hawthorne. I have come around to the view that the greatest of American writers was Nathaniel Hawthorne. He wrote *The Scarlet Letter* and a huge number of brilliant short stories. He is an expert on the Puritans and he takes their culture apart through a series of emblematic narratives. He gets to the heart of some of these psychological mythologies by telling stories that are very expressionistic. In 'The Birth Mark', an alchemist marries a very beautiful woman and he sees she has got a birth mark. He tells her, 'I could make you perfect, and it wouldn't hurt', and he nags and nags, and finally, right after they have been married, she says 'OK'. He starts a series of experiments in his laboratory and this thing starts to fade. It works. Just at the point of it disappearing altogether, leaving her perfect, without blemish, in his mind, she dies. And now she is perfect.

Some Wordsworth, I think would be essential on this course because there are writers – like Hawthorne and Wordsworth and Blake – who teach people about literature *in* their writing. And on this course, we can't afford to waste our time. We have to teach two things; we have to teach the stuff, we have to teach how to illuminate *all* of literature. I would have a project in this course, where each student, with the help of the teacher, would select a memory from her or his personal life, and turn it into a story, with whatever creative decisions they like. But this memory will be the seed of a narrative. That's how they'll see what the process is.

It's time. There are a lot of people out there who are unhappy with what is going on in universities. For instance, this young woman who was my student and who is now in the last year of her PhD, wrote to me and said that she's not looking to teach at university. She can't relate. She's going to go to a high school or a college, where literature can still be taught.

I have got over 60 people working for me in The Reader Organisation. They are all out reading with people, all day long. It's not formal teaching because there are no courses. But to go to a drug detox unit, as I will tomorrow morning and sit and read 'Infant Joy' and 'Infant Sorrow' for an hour, that's teaching. It's meeting people who are keen to discover some information; they want to change their lives.

This war in English departments is really a war on biology; they want to treat people as though they are not biological. It's dangerous. It's a kind of Nazi interpretation of people that doesn't pay any attention to their grounding in their own biology. It's like Conrad's *Heart of Darkness*, where there is a huge fear of the power of feelings. When people in authority are scared of the Heart of Darkness they want control over it. It reminds me how drums were banned here at one point – did you know that? Drums were banned by the government in Canada because the Native Americans used drums in their religion. They still have festival drums, it's really quite exciting, and the idea that they once couldn't do this is amazing.

In some schools in England students are not allowed to use the word 'I' in essays.

It's part of this tyranny. It's based on the notion that there isn't any 'I', but try and find out where the authority came from if not from there... I mean, if there is no 'I', who *is* in charge?

Would you describe yourself as a religious person, a spiritual person?

Maybe spiritual, not religious. I have a problem with authority... A colleague of mine wrote a book called *In Search of Authority*, which describes how people, in English, will always look for an authorised version and so they go through schools of criticism. But I don't want to describe the object as having some kind of inherent authority. It's obvious that as I read a novel something is going on that consists of a vastly complicated interaction, which is the story as composed by the author and by me.

When you first went into family therapy work, did you realise at that point that you were creating an alternative path for your literary work, or was it more a frustration with the university approach to literature?

I think it was both because I did it very deliberately. Something was happening – in my classrooms students were having emotional responses to books, and I encouraged them to have these responses – which was not popular where I was teaching, but I did do it. Then I happened to be able to take this training, to become a clinical member of the American Association for Marriage and Family Therapy. In Waterloo, where the university was, there was a training centre and they let me in. I had to talk my way in to it. The training took several years. Well it was part-time. I took one sabbatical for it, and then I did a whole series of courses and I was trained as a counsellor. It took years and years of hard work and it was wonderful work, I loved it. But I did always intend to join it to my involvement with literature, particularly with stories. So I did a lot of workshops on this, about the role of the therapist as editor. I could see myself playing a healing role in what I came to call a broken story. You can repair a broken story.

But you have got to be conscious of what's being read and written. What was the history of this? When was this happening?

This was in the seventies. The eighties. The nineties. I was an advocate for an approach that included psychology and medicine as well as the reading of books and poems. I was an advocate of what is called affective criticism. But the hostility I ran into bewildered me. People say there was blood on the walls in the faculty in the Humanities where I was. We had battles, I was under no illusion about this conflict; they *told* me what they thought of my approach. They didn't want me doing it; they said it was dangerous, my students would have nervous breakdowns, they didn't want affect.

They didn't want me getting involved with peoples' experiences. And yet at the same time there was a Professor in Manitoba, a Rabbi, and a Professor of Hebrew and Aramaic languages, and he took his students round to the different churches and places of worship, and he blindfolded them, because he wanted them to experience what was going on as a *whole* thing, the smells, sounds, spaces etc. Why wasn't that dangerous too? Why is that different as an experience to what I was doing with my students?

Reading is not part of our morality and it's not a kind of artificial therapy; it's part of our constructing a reality for ourselves, a world for ourselves.

POETRY

ALISON BRACKENBURY

From experience

I asked my grandfather, who spent
more time with flocks, fields, fine
mists than with sons, what he had learnt
was a true weather sign.
He sank in cloud,
cool pipe smoke curled,
rose up to darkened hills of mind,
tapped out, 'I allus watch the moon.'

I stand in my town's frost-locked street.
I wait for friends, their deep warm car.
I see the clouds' cliffs tear and part
to bays of blue, one drifting star.
Red rainbows ache
the light's chill lake.
'By, see them clouds! Snow's coming soon.'
He raps his pipe. I watch my moon.

For a friend, now running a radio station

A pocket of time was lent.
We left home. Country style
I ached to drive a hundred miles
while you had flown a continent.

Taut greyhounds, we worshipped the mind,
which can burn through heart and bone.
But the body is all we own.
We wasted so much time.

The sourer plotters said of you,
fresh from apartheid's wire and cards,
you thought no English rule was hard.
Invisible gates close too.

Let me swim through the senses' pool!
My beads from Africa, from you,
burned kingfisher, raw orange, blue.
You wore soft socks, kind navy wool.

You found, from river's fogs and chill,
your aunt's warm house in Wales.
In your voice, her songs sailed
over the settlers' gravel.

Your tastes looked plain: much tea,
thick, discreet biscuits. Fruit
fell into my mouth, sudden loot,
shocked fathers. For no heart slips free.

What did we do, after? Kind air
warmed. Wars flared. We vote
to shorten them. Words swill my throat.
You are the new Queen of the Air.

But you must think I cannot count,
that I have left one sense behind.
Remember a day of dark wind?
You opened my door, half-reeled out.

Wired jasmine was wreathing the room,
its white breath your childhood heat.
It died; you moved on. No defeat.
Scent spills from time's pocket, our home.

COUNTER-BLAST

A ROGUE PROLOGUE
A HEARTFELT PLEA FOR A BIT OF COMMON SENSE

Janet Suzman

A friend of long-standing, – I shall call her X in time-honoured fashion – suddenly declared her interest in the Earl of Oxford. Who he? I knew dimly that he'd been singled out by people who have nothing better to do than doubt Shakespeare's authorship of his own plays. Since everything about Shakespeare, his life and his genius, remains a profound mystery, the piling on of further obfuscations shot through with cant, piffle and deception seems to me a poor subject for deep analysis. Furthermore, to waste good millions on a lousy film to defend the indefensible, seems both profligate and time-wasting. Even spending my time on this counter-blast is slightly irritating. But I find myself wanting to defend the man from Stratford; the one person in the known universe who doesn't need my defence. Paradox is the name of the Shakespearian game, is it not? Having fallen in love with English long ago in a hot African schoolroom, I am honour-bound to declare my fealty to the man from Stratford; his authorship of his own plays and poems makes perfect sense to me while blasting those same senses to smithereens.

I knew this much about the time-wasters: that for many a decade Shakespeare's breathtaking talent and huge output has bamboozled the brains of mere mortals, and so the easiest way out of bamboozlement is to assign the entire canon to another, more conventionally educated, brain. Francis Bacon was suggested as author, by a great-great-great grand niece of his called Delia Bacon in the late nineteenth century. No one up to then had smelt a rat. Then Christopher Marlowe and Ben Jonson had their turn, but since there were little credibility flaws, such as talent, style, and timelines, the hapless Earl of Oxford was finally appointed instead. A pair of grand American novelists took up the cause, and most worryingly Sigmund Freud – a man whose language was not English but whose brain was amazed at the psychological accuracy of Shakespearian dramatic characters. To this day there is a group of Freudian psychoanalysts who meet every third Sunday in Hampstead to study those dramatic motivations in detail from the playtexts.

The reasons for Oxford's latter-day coronation seem tenuous bar that he lived almost but not quite concurrently with William, wrote a few poems of uneven quality, was rich and well connected, was patron of a theatre company for a time, talked occasionally to Queen Elizabeth when he wasn't being banished by her, but chiefly possessed a suitable geography in his life, having travelled both to the Continent and the Americas, as is the wont of young aristocrats. Oh, yes, and had a classical university education, learning his Latin and Greek at Oxbridge, which naturally makes him a genius. I joke.

Travel makes it possible, you see, to write plays set in foreign climes. For your Oxfordian, it's impossible for a writer to conjure up another world in the imagination; he has to have been there, which puts the entire range of science fiction into the rubbish-bin. I am not aware that Shakespeare ever offered up street maps of his towns, Rome, Verona or Padua, though he did mention the Rialto, the incredibly famous Venetian bridge. I guess because he'd heard of it. That's what Oxfordians require – topographical accuracy; the metaphor of the plays are quite beside the point.

You have to be a conspiracy theorist to imagine the Earl of Oxford secretly wrote thirty-seven plays performed and printed over a quarter of a century without being found out. And you have to be a snob if you hate it that the greatest poet the world has ever produced was born into the humble aldermanic classes of a provincial town.

JANET SUZMAN

So, not being a scholar or an academic, I hereby consider myself free to throw down the gauntlet unconstrained by the chivalry and accuracy of those noble professions. I'm a mere actor. I can rant all I like. And it is from the actor's standpoint only that I shall do so.

In 2011 a murky and far-fetched film was released – Sony-backed, shame on them wasting their money on such a bad subject – called *Anonymous*; the invented story of how this Earl of Oxford was the real author of the plays. No facts to back it up, just wild submissions and some quite good cinematography of the gloomy historical documentary kind. Roughly this is how their batty film version goes: Oxford was always secretly writing plays, having already written *Midsummer Night's Dream* when he was about eight years old and entranced with his own prodigiousness, he continued in secret. But how was he to get these works into the playhouses without revealing his blue blood? The Queen would have had him topped had she known. Thus Oxford, desperate for a theatrical conduit, singles out Ben Jonson, playwright, needing money for a reason I cannot now recall, and Ben is duly blackmailed and sworn to silence – a brilliant writer libelled beyond recognition.

Oxford could now feed his plays through Jonson's bribed hands to reach the actors. However, one day a doltish and illiterate member of the acting company – justify an illiterate actor to me please – namely one William Shakespeare, finds out about the deception and so Ben has to pay him clandestinely, courtesy of the rich earl, to keep his mouth shut. Oh, and for the use of his nice name. Thus it was that he, dim-witted Will, got all the kudos for the huge success of these plays.

Has it never occurred to this bunch of dreamers how such a daft plot might work in a busy theatre company? Their scenario works off torture and bribery anyway. There wouldn't be enough money in the universe to stop all the actors in a company from blabbing till Doomsday, let alone the masses of other people involved in a theatre company; the tirers delivering head dresses, the sewing women mending torn costumes, the butchers and bakers and candlestick-makers. No whispers and sniggers about such a plonking *modus operandi*, a deception stretching over twenty-five years? Did their William never crow in his cups about his secret benefactor and growing wealth? Did the Company never notice how illiterate Will had suddenly turned scribe, brandishing inky cue-sheets under their noses? Did no-one ever mark how re-writes – for re-writes there surely were – happened only after this William returned from a loo-break? We must assume the author earl was in the building that day skulking about in the gods ready for consultation. You think

"If they didn't blab they were inhuman,
and actors are human"

the cleaning-woman didn't spot him as she swept up vomit and hazel-nut shells? A conspiracy, you understand, demands silence from everyone; unattainable in a theatre company, with skittering boys and prying eyes on the loose in a building with no doors to shut on secrets. If they didn't blab they were inhuman, and actors are all human that's for sure.

The earl died in 1604 and Shakespeare lasted till 1616, but hey, no worries, the late plays secretly mature in the company cellar like bottles of vintage claret, to be broached one by one with a flourish when a new play is required. In the silly film a pile of the late plays are tremblingly handed by the dying earl to Ben Jonson for safe-keeping. Ben then manages to hide them in a tin trunk beneath the stage. For nine years those plays lie safe, un-discovered by prying prop-hands. Then the terrible Globe fire of 1613 happens, and lo! they are rescued by Ben. A sigh of relief when he notes that *Antony and Cleopatra* is sooty but all there for posterity. Well, whew! But this silliness hides a very serious point: if the Oxfordian bunch assume that the late plays could have been written early it beggars belief about their understanding of the maturing trajectory of not only this supreme mind, but any writer. It assumes a genius that not even a genius could have managed.

Here's Peter Brook writing vividly on this central question, the daily life of a busy theatre company, left entirely unaddressed by the Oxfordian illuminati:

We must never lose touch with the communal nature of theatre. An actor says to an author – 'This bit seems a bit long, couldn't we cut it?' or 'I haven't enough time for a costume change – could you write a soliloquy or a little

scene on the forestage to help?' Imagine a fake Shakespeare put on the spot? No-one smelled a rat amongst all those spiteful and jealous rivals? Even today, imagine a phoney writer. The cast would begin to notice and gossip about the fact that every time you ask something, the author slips into the wings with his cell phone.

In case anybody is still under the illusion that a complicated thing like a play just happens without rehearsal, here is corroboration from the introduction to Germaine Greer's *Shakespeare*:

Elizabethan popular drama was unique in Europe in that the playwrights insisted on absolute control. In the introduction to his verse translation (1610) of Thomas Tomkis's morality play, *Lingua*, Johannes Rhenanus described how such control was exercised. 'So far as actors are concerned they, as I noticed in England, are daily instructed, as it were in a school, so that even the most eminent actors have to allow themselves to be instructed by the dramatists, which arrangement gives life and ornament to a well-written play, so that it is no wonder that the English players (I speak of the skilled ones) surpass and have the advantage of others'.

You only have to hear the funniest scenes in the canon written about actors playing actors in the *Dream* to realise the author was familiar with the ways of – er – actors. It's written with love, sympathy and mockery all tumbled in a whole heap of theatrical 'nous'. Oh no! – sorry, Lord Oxford wrote it when still a mere lad, I quite forgot.

Greer continues of Hamlet's speech to the players: 'he gives precise instructions in the manner of delivery, "trippingly", not mouthing and grimacing or obscuring the matter with exaggerated gestures: "let those that play your clowns speak no more than is set down for them"' (3.2.38-9). A lot of ad-libbing must have gone on, there's a detectable rush of minor irritation at unruly actors. In the mouth of Hamlet, Shakespeare is simply reminding actors given to coarseness, that over-acting is a bore. He suggests an unadorned style of delivery, speedy, full of clarity, and no unnecessary gestures. It holds good today, and is the most difficult to achieve. Less is eternally more.

No novelist (Mark Twain, Henry James) working alone, nor diviner of new pathways into the human psyche (Freud), nor scholar feeling his way through patterns of writing can know how a company of actors must resolve difficulties 'fast and together', as Peter Brook describes the process. These three are the star names that hold to the Oxfordian view, and I am trying to think why. Freud was born into a poor family but it was a Jewish one so it struggled to ensure he was well educated. James was born into a rich one so he was OK. Twain made his adventurous way in the world after leaving school early, so he and Freud have a tenuously superficial commonality with Shakespeare's early life in the matter of relative poverty only.

Shakespeare's education at Stratford's grammar school – and it is far more likely than unlikely that he attended it – gave him a rigorous education in the classics and in rhetoric certainly well in advance of Twain's. Jonathan Bate comments that the level in these subjects reached when you left such a grammar school would be roughly equivalent to a first year at university now. There is evidence to show that other mercers of Stratford were well-educated and cultivated persons, and there is an extant letter written in Latin by a boy of eleven to his father who was a friend of the Shakepeares.

Conclusion? This illustrious trio's ignorance about how plays happen must be the deciding factor in their doubts about Stratford Shakespeare's abilities. No such excuse in the film in which a slew of brilliant actors take part, who surely know the process. But the film is so laboured in the liberties it takes with known history that one cannot be surprised, albeit irritated, at its convolutions with unknown history. Especially in regard to Queen Elizabeth; her inside knowledge of the deception, her endless pregnancies and an away-with-the-fairies, incredible incestuous liaison with her own son, (oh happy Freud!). It is brought vividly off by the brilliant Vanessa Redgrave whom we know likes embracing causes. Such is my admiration for her luminous, unforgettable acting that I must allow her some slack. A stab at this disarmingly louse-ridden Elizabeth was obviously irresistible to her.

However, she is accompanied in the film by two other stunning actors, Derek Jacobi and Mark Rylance, where my leeway screeches to a halt. Both are declared Oxfordians. I keep wondering exactly when their own professional experience went flying out the window, and why? We have seen a dozen times how thrillingly they can conjure up fantastical character studies of fictional persons, without ever having been crowned king or murdered a rival in real life. It's what actors do, for heaven's sakes, and Shakespeare was one too. Theirs is a powerful gift that allows them to travel in the mind to any exotic land, to conjure up a brilliantly believable *somebody*, apparelled in clothes never worn in their own daily life, speaking in accents not native to them, comporting themselves in ways quite foreign to their own hearth, uttering thoughts way beyond any they have ever conceived. It's called imagination. And

"Shakespeare was not just clever"

these two great actors were born somewhere in the British Isles of parents as ordinary as schoolteachers and tobacconists. It's called talent. And imagination is the central component of it. Rylance's naturalness with verse is supremely compelling, almost time-warping the listener into Hamlet's presence.

However William Shakespeare was not just clever but a rarer thing, a genius with a mind that no other being has come near to. Genius implies a huge capacity for concentration, for hard work, for long hours, for a voracious mind. He was a poet/actor, applying his sky-wide imagination to his trade in the company of just such fellows as Rylance and Jacobi. He wrote, they performed. All invented, magicked, given outsize reality by the power of his gift, goading his colleagues into ever more complex and responsive life onstage as his flexibility with ideas and with verse matured.

Heminge and Condell felt moved to collate and publish the plays they had performed over the years, making a public tribute to their dead Friend. No hint or sniff there of the deception that the Oxfordians favour. The First Folio of 1623 is a loving tribute, righting the wrong of manuscripts previously 'deformed by the frauds and stealthes of injurious impostors'. How strange it is that Jacobi and Rylance, hundreds of years later, with their outstanding acting instincts should embrace such a haughty view of the man who has made them as big as they are.

It seems to me that the entire history of the human race is the history of the immense struggle to move *upwards*; to overcome migration, to rise above bourgeois braces, to free oneself from the shackles of poverty, prejudice, and the Pale. Is it just my left-leaning propensities that recoil from the Oxfordian view that only an aristocrat can enter the soul of a king, or that only a university-trained mind can display such a ready wit? Or that an aristocratic mind is so unfathomable that a stranger to the class couldn't emulate its distinction? More interesting than a man born into privilege would be the creative anonymity of a most private man quietly observing London's throngs, the accents of strangers, the jargon of professionals, meeting people from all social classes and backgrounds; devouring books, poetry, plays, tracts, being as curious about everyone and everything as an artist should be in the excitement and turmoil of this greatest of river cities.

How's this for a revealing clue: Antony to Cleopatra: 'and all alone tonight we'll wander through the streets and note the qualities of people'? That's what he did, I have no doubt. Will Shakespeare strolled the streets of London, observing the life around him, invisible, unremarked, an ordinary man. It's tempting to think this fragmentary insight into his unreported life might be the sole piece of (whisper it) autobiography we dare infer from the entire canon.

After a youth spent in a cultural backwater, largely devoid of live theatre although very alive to the violence and avarice of living – Johannesburg – I can vouch for the joys of Learning Very Quickly once plunged into the magical maelstrom of London. I soon absorbed the fell gradations of the English class system, picked up the going lingo, met hundreds of foreigners, tried out my school French with them, and worse, my Cockney, generally adjusted seamlessly into ways that were strange to my upbringing. I'm no genius; it's the story of London.

Everyone is changed by it, and charged up by it. You expand your experience of human nature by leaps and by bounds, and chiefly, if you're an actor, you observe and you listen, you listen hard to the myriad accents around you; it's grist to your mill, it's your bread and butter. A modest demeanour and a Warwickshire accent, honestly come by, would have afforded a precious ordinariness to Shakespeare. The gentleness of his nature, mentioned repeatedly by admirers – we have at least a dozen known contemporaries of his who knew him well and who mention him both as author and actor; a continuous series of traces left from 1592 until his death in 1616 – would have drawn people out and his unforced interest would surely have invited conversation. He sounds like a charmer.

Try to imagine the vigilance it would take for an earl to be amongst the vulgar, trying hard not to be recognised, adjusting his courtly accent, his refined manners, his entitled demeanour. I am assuming he had one, as this foreigner has noticed that the aristocracy can't help revealing its origins in casual encounter. Even our friendly demotic Prince William is marked out by his perfectly ironed clothes. The Queen of Egypt and her lover strolling through the streets of Alexandria hoping not to be rumbled offer a sense of playfulness that is quite lacking in the relentlessly deceitful scenario of the Oxfordians.

So, in the absence of the sort of hard evidence suggested above that would satisfy those who doubt the references to a living breathing writer called Shakespeare, I joyfully take recourse, not being myself a scholar, in the pragmatism of science, to flag up my disdain for the conspiracy theorists. The major principle I propose to invoke to swat away the baseless buzzing of the sceptics is known as Occam's razor, meaning roughly 'simplest is best'. I have sometimes invoked it for acting students when I teach – er – Shakespeare. The following elegant explanation, for those of us who don't do science, I owe to my son, Josh, who is a physicist:

The idea is that you always have a choice of different explanations [for a scientific observation]. Occam's razor says you should choose the explanation that involves the smallest number of concepts or 'things'. Suppose you see a rainbow. There are an infinite number of ways to explain it. It could be that there's a leprechaun making the colours, but the leprechaun is invisible. It could be that on a rainy day there is a special substance in the air that makes colours when the sun hits it. Or, it could be that sunlight is composed of many different colours, and rain-drops in the air split them up. The last one is the 'science' explanation because it satisfies Occam's razor. It's the simplest explanation because it doesn't add any

new concepts (like leprechauns or special substances), it just uses pre-existing concepts (light, the physics of refraction in water). Somehow it answers the original question (what makes a rainbow?) without simultaneously creating more questions (where do leprechauns come from? Why can't I see them?)

'I think it's interesting,' Josh continues, 'because ultimately Occam's razor is an aesthetic principle, which you can only really justify by saying that simpler theories are just "more beautiful"'. In some sense all of science can be viewed as a rather arbitrary attempt to satisfy this desire for beauty in simplicity. And if you don't sign up to the idea that simple is beautiful, well then you are quite justified in not signing up to science.

Well, there you go, I am signing up wholeheartedly to the idea that in science, in art, in life too, simplest is best. The poor Earl of Oxford's life, such as we know it, is way too complicated, not to mention too short, to have fitted into the sneaky diurnal disguise devised for him. Writing, directing, and acting in a slew of your own plays, in a company of performers who know you well, in a town abuzz with gossip and rivalry, for a quarter of a century is really more than enough for any one man to have accomplished. To have somehow feigned all this, God knows how, without being rumbled, simply beggars belief. And what about the collaborations, becoming increasingly clear with closer analysis, with Middleton, Fletcher, and other dramatists of the age? Even the most eager Oxfordian could not write the scene where that happened. I am signing up wholeheartedly to the idea that in science, in art, in life too, simplest is best. Occam's exquisite Razor comes deliciously to hand to slash to shreds all the barmy complications: Oxford did not write the plays. William Shakespeare of Stratford is the man who knows the quiet industry of creation and the hurly-burly of staging it. It's as simple as that. Otherwise we are truly away with the leprechauns.

POETRY

THE OLD POEM

Brian Nellist

Thomas Nashe (1567–c.1601)
from *Summer's Last Will and Testament*

Fair summer drops, droop men and beasts therefore;
So fair a summer look for never more.
All good things vanish, less than in a day,
Peace, plenty, pleasure, suddenly decay.
   Go not yet away, bright soul of the sad year;
   The earth is hell when thou leav'st to appear.

What, shall those flowers, that decked thy garland erst,
Upon thy grave be wastefully dispersed?
O trees, consume your sap in sorrow's source;
Streams, turn to tears your tributary course.
   Go not yet hence, bright soul of the sad year;
   The earth is hell when thou leav'st to appear.

ON *SUMMER'S LAST WILL AND TESTAMENT* (1600)

In his dream vision of the future, *News from Nowhere*, William Morris has a character called Dick who explains why he prefers the festivities of hay to the corn festival; 'for then the year is beginning to fail, and one cannot help having a feeling behind all the gaiety, of the coming of the dark days, and the shorn fields and empty gardens'. The dreamer who is delighted by this happy Arts and Crafts world protests but Dick replies, 'I mean that I am part of it all and feel the pain as well as the pleasure in my own person'. Forward is also backwards to Morris, and Dick's pain expresses that intimate vision of man with natural process that for the writer seemed lost by 1890 when the book appeared. Like the 'rise of the middle-classes' in old-fashioned histories that supposed loss has always been happening, however, in the gap between the sophisticated town and the conservative countryside, not least in this play by Thomas Nashe. More like an entertainment or a masque it was probably written in 1592 for presentation before Archbishop Whitgift's household at Croydon and during a plague year when London theatres were closed. Will Summers, court jester to Henry VIII, is resurrected to offer mordant comments on the debate between lavish, generous summer and austere Puritan winter, on the clumsiness of the actors and the learned digressions. Typically of Nashe it sends up what it also honours.

It includes a sequence of songs starting with this one for autumn. It scarcely needs comment, though we might note that the summer had been hot that year. The line that always stays in the memory is 'Go not yet away bright soul of the sad year'. It's partly the effect of that 'yet', longing for summer to be extended, like Keats's 'To Autumn' but expressed as though begging a friend to stay. And there he is, a frail old man, at the start of the play supported by Autumn and Winter, to make us 'feel the pain as well as the pleasure' in our own persons. It's the music of the line which picks it out and, let me be pedantic, a trochee followed by scrambling anapaest and lingering over a spondee, a foot with two equally-stressed syllables, 'bright soul'. Most of us are at least a little subject to SAD so, even though we adjust to dark days, we can recognize the accusation that earth becomes dull in the general retreat of nature before the onslaught. The sap retreats from the twigs; 'fall of the leaf', the Fall as Americans abbreviate it, was the old word for the turn of the year. The imagery of the poem and the play works on many levels and over long stretches as with Shakespeare.

MINTED

PRACTICAL POETRY FOR LIFE

Edited by Brian Nellist

The banks may not be lending at this moment but what Ruskin called 'The King's Treasury' is always open and generous. It is his image for great writing and when we enter it with desire to understand fuelled by our needs it lends us inexhaustible riches. We think and feel more deeply because the gold is not simply deposited in our minds but it finances our own activity of mind and spirit...

This is a travel brochure to encourage your own exploration and there are plenty of anthologies to take things further. The brief characterisations of what's happening in the lines is there to suggest their usefulness because that's what great writing is; useful.

Published 27th September; £5.00
Get it through The Reader Organisation
www.thereader.org.uk

MAKING USE OF DEATH

Raymond Tallis

e may believe that medicine will exert increasing control over disease and over the ageing process and the world may become a safer place, as we pacify nature and (even) human nature. Death is inevitable. We cannot do anything about it. And so we had better make it work for us. For this we need to see it clearly, to live in its presence.

Death is most obviously made visible to us in those we have known and see no longer with us: erstwhile companions of the daylight who are now in the sunless realm. The dead occupy that outside of life – of the sum total that we designate by the term 'the human world' – to which we can refer so easily that we do not notice or admit, that it is too difficult to imagine. The dead who may come to our aid are not necessarily those to whom we were close, those whose passing caused us a grief that is always fresh, nor the more remote dead, those who were always only names, or categories or numbers. Rather, I am thinking of what we may call the middle-ground dead: the colleague you nodded to every morning over ten or twenty years, the man you used to chat with from time to time over a pint; the fellow committee member who once winked at a crucial time in a meeting. They are large enough to be real but not so large that their passing empties us. They are real in that we have an overpowering sense that they shared with us the million lights and shadows of the human world.

I cannot resist quoting from Rilke's great poem 'Experience of Death' because it seems entirely to the point I am trying to make. It is addressed to someone who has died:

> **But, as you went, a segment of reality**
> **flashed in upon our stage by that same crevice**
> **through which you passed: the green of real verdure,**
> **the real sunshine and the real wood.**

It is in this spirit that we might remember those who were as alive and complex as we are, who now are simply *not*; those whose lives were as unimaginably huge as ours, who filled worlds that simply popped. This is the spirit of Hamlet's vision when he looks at the skulls turned up by the gravedigger's spade: 'That skull had a tongue in it, and could sing once'.

Or when he reflects on the transience of glory and of those gigantic presences who strode the face of the earth:

> **Imperious Caesar, dead and turn'd to clay**
> **Might stop a hole to keep the wind away.**
> **O, that that earth which kept the world in awe**
> **Should patch a hole to expel the winter flaw!**

You can read into these passages many things: mockery of the mighty or the important, or the self-important, who are fallen; or horror at our common fate. But there is something deeper: perhaps not for Hamlet, for whom they were simply a way of distracting himself from his disgust and bitterness and rage at the world. That deeper something is astonishment, wonder. Our reduction to our rotting bodies, our heads reduced to the simplicity of the skull, highlight by contrast the scale, the complexity of ourselves and our lives. The cognitive balloon that is our world, the immeasurably long journey that is the most everyday of everyday lives that leaves its trail in rooms, streets, cities, fields, mountains, countries – gone with the most inter-mittent of traces, fading fast:

> **There's another: why may that not be the skull of a**
> **lawyer? Where be his quiddities now, his quillets, his**
> **cases, his tenures and his tricks? Why does he suffer**
> **this rude knave now to knock him about the sconce**

with a dirty shovel, and will not tell him of his action of battery? Hum! This fellow might be in's time a great buyer of land, with his statutes, his recognizances, his fines, his double vouchers, his recoveries: is this the fine of his fines, and the recovery of his recoveries, to have his fine pate full of fine dirt? Will his vouchers vouch him no more of his purchases, and double ones too, than the length and breadth of a pair of indentures? The very conveyance of his lands will hardly lie in this box; and must the inheritor himself have no more, ha?

This may seem a strange source of good cheer, not too distant from the gloom and terror of Pascal's meditation:

Imagine a number of men in chains, all under sentence of death, some of whom are butchered each day in the sight of others; those remaining see their own condition in that of their fellows, and looking at each other with grief and despair await their turn. This is an image of the human condition.

But against this we have to reflect on the fact that there is a human condition. That this is so invites us to think about the mystery of our existence and the infinitely complex texture of everyday life, and the dizzying fact that we who live this condition are aware of it, can think about it, and articulate it. Outliving is a privilege that puts the gift of living in italics.

Thinking of the deaths of those others is a way of approaching the least imaginable of all deaths – our own – and of trying to conceive the inconceivable: the cessation of our own existence, of we who are at this moment trying to conceive of this event. Those others who have gone before us offer a virtual vantage point from which we can look upon our own lives as if from the outside; so that we can see this morning, as it were in a glass cabinet, its comings and goings from the viewpoint of no day. From this outside, the sense that we *are* now; that we are in the light, encompassed by a known world seething with possibility; that we pay shared attention to a place in which we are gathered, in which our separate histories are convergent – and how complex those histories are; that we are able to listen, to think, to move, to plan, to hope, to bring about; that we can act in a theatre whose complexity is infinite; that we accept as a taken-for-granted norm all that history has shaped; that we are accustomed to ourselves, to our tone of voice, our twinges, the offices we occupy, the expectations that are placed on us, the language we speak, and so on: from this vantage point the luminous wonder of daily life may become visible, unpeeled.

This is nothing more or less than a gloss on E. M. Forster's profound observation: 'Death destroys a man, but the idea of death saves him.' Of course, the idea of death is the driver of great art. As Tolstoy said, 'whatever an artist is thinking of, he is thinking of his own death'. The sense of finitude animates a desperate desire to make a deeper, more coherent, sense of things, to seize hold of it in its greatness, to be equal in consciousness to the great world in which we find ourselves, of which we are conscious in a piecemeal, sequential, fragmented, small-world way. But it can work for those of us who are not artists. The idea of death is a threat, a goad and an inspiration. And its power is available to all of us who aim to live abundantly.

There could be no more potent way of awakening yourself to the wonder of the world than by imagining it in your own absence, as something looked back upon, looked at from the outside of all outsides that is death. This is a viewpoint that removes the cognitive burqa in which our busy, preoccupied, consciousness is wrapped. *Lux demonstrat umbra*: the shadow reveals the light. Or as was once said, 'In the cold waters of Lethe, you will remember the warm earth above' – this place, this day – 'meant a thousand suns'. In death's dark mirror, or in the dark mirror of imagined death, the light of daylight seems more luminous, more inexplicable, more precious. In the dazzled vision of one who has looked into and then away from undifferentiated darkness may grow a wonder that will survive the busy glance that dismisses it as self-indulgent, childish, affected or insincere, and see that it is true to the bitter and joyful mystery of our lives.

This is an abridged version of an essay which appears in Raymond Tallis's *In Defence of Wonder* (Acumen, 2012; ISBN 978-1-84465-525-0). Reprinted with the kind permission of the author.

POETRY

JOHN LEVETT

Sexing Skeletons

The long bones and the pelvis are our clues
Now flesh is an abstraction, now the skin,
The coloured eye, the philtrum, lips and nose
Shrink back to leave just teeth stuck in the grin.

We mix-and-match them, pair them up to find
Who goes with who in this new afterlife,
And so long dead they surely will not mind;
We sort the bones for husband, bones for wife,

Their skulls, their jaws dropped open for old wine
Or maggots in dead tongues that wagged to prize
The sexiness of talus, sternum, spine
Time strips and agricultures pulverize.

We catalogue them, lay them side by side,
The disarticulated made to stir,
To find, deep in their carbon, ossified,
This bias for the male we disinter.

So even dead some women, second best,
Are dug up, disassembled, reassigned
And rattled by each wrong, bone-headed guess
Amongst the ribs and hips they leave behind.

Our x-rays catch them as they incandesce,
Stripped bare, irradiated, cheated twice,
Now light years from the rags of their last dress
And held up to the lamp in sacrifice.

ESSAY

'FROM SULLEN EARTH'

Grace Farrington
(with Philip Davis and Josie Billington)

This essay takes another look at data originally collected for a study investigating the benefits of reading in relation to depression. I am going to focus on just one of the Get Into Reading transcripts; the group are reading a great poem (a Shakespeare sonnet) and a good session unfolds. The transcript captures the live feel of group members' responses both to the text and each other. Certain moments in the transcript, highlighted below, indicate both the need for breakthrough and what makes it happen. The project worker's interventions are noted, and attention is drawn to the ongoing process of deciding whether or not, and how, to intervene in the course of discussions around a poem.

The group meets in a mental-health drop-in centre in an area of Liverpool suffering high levels of deprivation and long-term unemployment. There are five members present, to whom fictional names have been given to preserve anonymity. Each has a confirmed diagnosis of depression, with several also struggling with anxiety. In a couple of the women this is expressed via an almost non-stop chatter, whilst with the others it is perhaps what makes them very quiet. Of the three women, one is in her eighties and recently widowed, there is a single mother with some learning disabilities, and also a middle-aged woman who is new to the group, presenting herself as an 'avid', experienced reader. The two men are more self-contained, and appreciate each other's company particularly since they tend to lack confidence in the group context. Meeting for the third time, with attendance having already varied each week, there is as yet much that is unsettled about what this group will become. The project worker takes this early opportunity to introduce a Shakespeare sonnet, which in comparison to the one poem that has been read in the group previously, 'Leisure' by W. H. Davies, is likely to be a challenge. The group is given a guarantee however: though at first sight the poem seems difficult, i) they will get through it, and ii) it will prove to be worth their while. The project worker, confident in the poem, reads:

> **When, in disgrace with Fortune and men's eyes,**
> **I all alone beweep my outcast state,**
> **And trouble deaf heaven with my bootless cries,**
> **And look upon myself and curse my fate –**
> **Wishing me like to one more rich in hope,**
> **Featur'd like him, like him with friends possess'd,**
> **Desiring this man's art and that man's scope,**
> **With what I most enjoy contented least;**
> **Yet in these thoughts myself almost despising**
> **Haply I think on thee, and then my state,**
> **Like to the lark at break of day arising**
> **From sullen earth, sings hymns at heaven's gate:**
> **For thy sweet love remember'd such wealth brings**
> **That then I scorn to change my state with kings.**

Margaret is the first to break the silence that follows.

Margaret: **That is very conflicting. You know, at the very beginning it's really down and out, and yet at the end it's on top of the world. Just in the matter of those –**
Project worker: **There is these two movements in the poem isn't there?**

Margaret: **Yes. Don't know why you bother living at the beginning and yet at the end, he has got everything to live for. A complete turnaround.**

Project worker: **And it turns around by his having a thought of something else, someone else.**

Linda: **By having the thought of something else. Think of thee.**

Project worker: **Yes, line 10.**

Already both Margaret and Linda have found a way *into* the poem: getting in is always the first stage to be achieved. Margaret has grasped the implications of this section – 'down and out' for example is a quite accurate spin-off of the poem's 'outcast state' in line 2 – but her reliance on quickly intelligent colloquialisms does not always show where she is getting her thoughts *from* in the poem. Still, the phrase 'and yet at the end' which she uses twice to get to the second half of her sentences suggests she has internalised the structural key to the poem in lines 9, and 10 ('yet', 'haply', 'and then'). Linda has usefully located the turning point. This is like real reading, before the words of the poem get replaced by more everyday terms. More of this pointing – this deictic reference – will be needed as the discussion progresses.

The project worker reads through the poem again in order to give those in the group who have not yet spoken another chance to take it in.

Beryl: **About a man with nothing isn't it. Or could be somebody who has lost everything, you know their home, their fortune: in disgrace with fortune and men's eyes.**

Margaret: **He is really feeling sorry for himself. He feels as much as though he is like an outcast on an island. As though, just on an island by himself. He is crying for help. Just standing shouting and there is nobody, nobody there to listen to him.**

Beryl's 'or' allows her to improve upon her initial statement with a second thought. It is not just that the man has 'nothing', like

Margaret's down-and-out. Margaret's image on the other hand of the 'outcast on an island', via the step up 'as though', goes beyond the mere paraphrase of 'feeling sorry for himself' to get to a language closer to that of the poem. Her (repeated) use of the term 'as though' is like Beryl's 'or': permission to guess, an enabler for the imagination. Re-using the adjective 'outcast' now, as a noun, Margaret attempts to refigure to herself the 'state' of the first nine lines.

With the second reading the group has started to do better at *staying in* the poem. There follows a short period in which the project worker helps the group to work chronologically, line-by-line, through it. Upon reaching the sestet however, and again coming upon the change that takes place there, Don starts to become excited.

> *Don*: **He doesn't feel sorry for himself either. He comes out of his depression and his anger towards the world.**

Don rarely speaks. He has a pronounced stutter. But his use of the phrasal verb 'come out of' seems to reinforce the poem's sense of a 'state' as a real dimension, where the speaker is stuck '*in* these thoughts' (line 9). When the group members' language, even in paraphrase, begins to become inflected by the language of the poem, the project worker knows something is happening.

The project worker, needing now to re-experience the break-through that the poem makes in its second half, asks if there is anyone who would like to give a final reading of the poem. Don despite his stutter, volunteers for the first time, manifestly emboldened by his speech a minute ago. He reads carefully and successfully, and is answered by the group.

> *Project worker*: **Thank you Don, beautifully read.**
> *Douglas*: **Very good.**
> *Margaret*: **Thank you, Don.**

Beryl is still glancing over the poem as she says:

Beryl: **I hate Shakespeare, I can't stand him. No I really don't like Shakespeare.**

The project worker, somewhat shocked by the violence of this outburst though having heard similar complaints before, provides Beryl with the option to explain further: 'Why is it you don't like him?'

Beryl: **I just don't like him, I don't like the verse, I don't like his poetry, I just don't like Shakespeare. When we were doing it at school it was absolutely boring I couldn't stand it. But 'haply I think on thee and then my state like the lark at break of day rising' – isn't that a beautiful verse.**
Project worker: **'Rising from sullen earth' – sullen earth was what the first half of the poem was about, back for a moment**
Beryl: **Isn't that lovely, isn't that lovely. I don't really like him, but that is beautiful.**

'I just don't' is a formulation the project worker knows from experience as the reductive opposite of 'it's as though': these are little indicators of attitude and response to meaning. But Beryl's instinct for the part of the poem that is 'beautiful' has made the difference. As she feels the movement of the poem from within the lines – the 'lark at break of day arising' – this movement gets into her, and lifts her. It is significant that '*beautiful*' then becomes 'isn't that *lovely*', for all the 'I don't *like*', again repeated. Surely Beryl might admit that if she is finding this verse to be 'lovely' then her previously held prejudice has been discounted? But as the project worker is weighing this up she decides that the priority for what she says next is not principally to uphold the status of Shakespeare the writer. It is to join Beryl in appreciating that which has made this sonnet worth reading. 'Beautiful isn't it.'

As Beryl comes upon the beauty of the verse, it is as though she is encountering not just the beauty of it but the sheer surprise of the thing itself felt for the first time again. 'I am actually –'

she says, and the words that follow, although lost amongst other voices, carry the tone of 'I am actually taken aback'. It is as if the surprise has shifted her out of a self-limiting mind-set. Having created an opening from within the poem, Beryl's response encourages other members of the group in turn to look at this 'bit' for longer.

> *Margaret*: **Like the lark, you know singing first thing in the morning: it's a new beginning.**
> *Linda*: **From the sullen earth sings hymns at heaven's gate.**
> *Beryl*: **That's what the lark does doesn't it, it goes up to heaven. Larks sing right up there you can't even see them. They go right up, they sing at heaven's gate. You can't even see them, but you can hear them.**
> *Project worker*: **So instead of those 'bootless cries' that weren't making any impact, now we can hear singing! Instead of the sullen earth too, that final downer in the poem.**

Use of the third person 'he' has faded from the discussion, 'you' indicating that we are no longer in the secondary realm merely of talking and thinking *about* the poem. Beryl's earlier repetition of lines 10 and 11 made what she had noticed about the poem – the manner and feel of it – *happen*. There seems now a sense with each of the group members that the poem is happening – and happening through them – as they speak. Margaret, positioning herself within the poem's present, recognises the feeling of it being daybreak (line 11): 'it's a new beginning' in other senses too. For Beryl it is as if she has come imaginatively into the presence of the lark; not that she can see it with her eyes, 'but you can hear them'. This kind of activating of the imagination has started to happen in multiple ways – including Linda's creative misreading of 'sudden' for 'sullen' (quietly corrected by the project worker) – as though the group have tapped into a new energy source.

Such energy and prompting towards activity, partly activated by Don, is not just something that the group members have found within themselves. It is more that it is called out of them by the poem. An ease of movement is released in Beryl for example, quite without either her intending it, or the project worker having intervened to engineer it. It is effortless. This is where the effect of beauty contrasts with the strategies of therapy. A self-help book exhorts the reader: 'Getting out of depression takes effort', and of course this is true in very real, practical ways. Yet it is as if there is another way, another language even, one which is demonstrated here with the unforced arrival of beauty. Don, at the end of the session, comments on the poem: 'It sounds a lot better now', his initial response having been, 'I just don't understand quite a lot of it'.

In fact the encounter with a beautiful object, whether it be the song of a lark, the lines of a poem, or Don's reading of them, causes the issue of how a person might feel about him- or herself to be left to one side. Beauty lifts people out of self-absorption, and away from the self-conscious issues and problem-solving methods of therapy. It has vitality, a lift like that of the poem's change, but no set agenda. We become interested instead in something or someone else with which or whom we can fall in love. Generosity seems to be a natural response both to the beautiful and the loved.

The Powercut
Pleshley 8-12 April 2002

When gloom sets in and I feel old and dim,
The candle glows and flickers, real and warm,
And I can wait. The Powercut will end.

The light went out, not switched, just stopped,
And left a blackness, cold and dead.
Absence of fridge-hum, household noises
Intensified the sense of isolation.
Echoes of light from passing cars sent
Cataracts from wall to floor
And left the darkness deeper.

Then as the bat-black windows blurs to grey,
Fear lessens. The candles and some matches
Are remembered in a kitchen drawer.
The candle glows and flickers, real and warm,
And I can wait.

Margaret Wickham

THE READING REVOLUTION

BUPA CARE HOME
NATIONAL CREATIVE WRITING COMPETITION

Margaret Wickham's winning poem conveys a strong sense of a real experience, and its ability to express this seems a simple property, but is ultimately a defining and triumphant one. Although still undoubtedly an accomplished piece at a glance, the poem's real power and creation of atmosphere is revealed when the lines are spoken. It was this quality which so impressed and moved those judging the competition entries, and also those present when 'The Powercut' was chosen as the poem to be read at the start of a weekly team meeting at The Reader Organisation. It seemed pertinent and vital, really, that the winner of a creative writing competition connected to Get Into Reading should have its full potential realised through being read aloud.

Ellen Perry

Ellen Perry, Aaron Eastwood and Michael McGrath were interns at The Reader Organisation March–June 2012. They selected 'The Powercut' from over 50 entries to a BUPA care home national creative writing competition.

THE READING REVOLUTION

DIARIES OF THE READER ORGANISATION

Patrick Fisher

I t has been almost a year since I packed my bags in Liverpool and, with a folding table and pack of 5 Mars bars in hand (thanks colleagues!), ventured north to begin a three-year Get Into Reading project in Glasgow.

As a Reader-in-Residence in three schools, my working week breaks down as four days of delivery and one day of recording and preparation. In Glasgow, schools are grouped in clusters called Learning Communities; often one high school and several feeder primaries from the same area. My project is set in the St Mungo's Learning Community, spending one day delivering one-to-ones and groups in Sacred Heart and St Anne's Primary Schools and two days in St Mungo's Academy. The emphasis is on the transition between primary and secondary school so almost all of the children I read with are in P7, the last year of primary school, or S1, the first year of secondary. To have a constant event in their lives is particularly important here as Calton, the main catchment area for St Mungo's, is statistically the most deprived area in Scotland. A report into poverty in *The Scotsman* newspaper stated that a child born in Calton is three times more likely to suffer heart disease, four times as likely to be hospitalised and ten times as likely to grow up in a workless household as a child in the city's prosperous western suburbs. Calton also has the lowest male life expectancy in Scotland (the low 50s), with a BBC Scotland report highlighting that, partly due to poor diet, crime, alcohol and drug abuse, life expectancy in Calton is lower than in some areas of Iraq or the Gaza Strip. For many families and homes here, a reading culture has never existed.

My first twelve months have been about establishing relationships with stories and poems, and with each other, that can grow for the whole three-year term. I deliver twenty sessions reaching over 280 children each week, through seven one-to-ones, ten small groups, two after-school clubs and one whole-school group. The latter in particular has had a huge impact on the presence of the project in the school as everyone, children and staff, is aware of the work and all have connected to a text, be it poetry or prose, positively in some way. Now as I walk through the school, or even ride the local buses, children will stop to say hello and ask with genuine relish what we will be reading this week.

For many, this has been the first time outside of a classroom that a story has been read and shared with them. Even holding a book or poem has been ground-breaking; initial evaluation showed that only three children had books of any description at home. Despite this lack of familiarity, I have met almost no resistance from the children when offered the chance to share a story. Even those sceptical about how reading for pleasure would match up to the joys of Xbox Live or watching a film have found something of immense worth in our sessions. In the primary schools, where emotional responses are often raw and unfiltered, one highlight has been the collective jumping up and down with uncontrollable joy and laughter at the quirks of language in *The Monster Under the Bed* by Kevin Dyer: 'No, jammy crusts you've dropped under the kitchytable and squashygrapes that have rollied under the washy-sheen', followed by every child spontaneously reading aloud together to be as close to the story as possible. In St Mungo's it has been a chance for children to escape the more serious expectations of the world around them and an opportunity perhaps to voice ideas or feelings they lack the confidence to express elsewhere. Across all schools though, the biggest success has been enabling the discovery of reading as an event, accessible and fun, that can be shared with friends in school and family at home. To be a part of those first, exciting moments in a reader is a real privilege and one that I look forward to continuing next year.

FRANK COTTRELL BOYCE,
THE UNFORGOTTEN COAT –
WRITTEN FOR
THE READER
ORGANISATION'S
OUR READ 2011 –
IS SHORTLISTED
FOR *THE GUARDIAN*
CHILDREN'S
FICTION PRIZE.

**THE UK'S FIRST
PROFESSOR OF READING**
FRANK HAS BEEN APPOINTED
PROFESSOR OF READING
AND COMMUNICATION
AT LIVERPOOL
HOPE
UNIVERSITY

THE READING REVOLUTION

BEGINNING

Casi Dylan

n my final shared reading session at START creative arts and wellbeing centre in Salford we read T. S. Eliot for the whole two hours. I was moving to a new city, handing over the longstanding group to a volunteer. I felt the need to mark the occasion, to let this last time together stand for what we had been doing for the past eighteen months. We read the end of 'Little Gidding' from *Four Quartets*:

> **What we call the beginning is often the end**
> **And to make an end is to make a beginning.**
> **The end is where we start from. And every phrase**
> **And sentence that is right (where every word is at home,**
> **Taking its place to support the others,**
> **The word neither diffident nor ostentatious,**
> **An easy commerce of the old and the new,**
> **The common word exact without vulgarity,**
> **The formal word precise but not pedantic,**
> **The complete consort dancing together)**
> **Every phrase and every sentence is an end and a**
> **   beginning,**
> **Every poem an epitaph. And any action**
> **Is a step to the block, to the fire, down the sea's throat**
> **Or to an illegible stone: and that is where we start.**
> **We die with the dying:**
> **See, they depart, and we go with them.**
> **We are born with the dead:**

See, they return, and bring us with them.
The moment of the rose and the moment of the yew-tree
Are of equal duration. A people without history
Is not redeemed from time, for history is a pattern
Of timeless moments. So, while the light fails
On a winter's afternoon, in a secluded chapel
History is now and England.

So much in this reflected our own experience, not only in the consciousness that there we were simultaneously making an end and a beginning of the group. (Pam likes that '*make* an end', '*make* a beginning': 'it seems very active somehow.') It was that we had been together engaged with so many words, building of ourselves the capacity to recognise 'where every word is at home, / Taking its place to support the others.' ('That's spot on, that', says Barry, 'spot on.') And the poem extended our experience in its depth and multiplicity – all those *everys* – disallowing any sense of neatness at our ending. ('Every poem an epitaph... Any action takes us further 'down the sea's throat' – that's scary that,' says Tom, '...and beautiful.') As big, scary, beautiful as the conversation felt for those two hours, what I loved most was the specificity of that final line, its particular cast of light: 'History is now and England.' It spoke to me of what we had built in *this* room on *this* street in *this* particular corner of the city. The room which, when it was not our reading room on Friday mornings, was also used for reiki, massage, creative writing, staff meetings. Not only had we built a place for ourselves and our reading there – we had re-built it, between 10am and 12 noon every week.

All this is in my mind because I have recently started a new group in another new city: every Thursday lunchtime you'll find me in Glasgow Women's Library leading 'Unwind with a Book'. Last week there were nine of us: we read Katherine Mansfield and Anne Brontë; the group brought lunch to share. Since my time in Salford the peripatetic nature of running courses has meant that I was never in one place long enough to run a weekly group. But now 'Unwind with a Book' offers me not only a chance to re-engage with regular practice and a growing community; it offers a measure by which I can observe development in my own practice and thought. The very act of 'beginning' strikes me as compelling: it often raises concerns in those who have just completed Read to Lead training, heading off to set up their own groups. Full of will and energy to get going, there is something in the thought of (re)presenting shared reading to a new audience – prospective commissioner, group member, colleague – that stalls them. 'What's best to put on the poster?' 'What's the first thing I should say in the group?' Shared reading means something to them, and they want to be true to that meaning.

So much has happened even before the beginning. To be in the position to begin running a group, you will inevitably have developed your own deep sense of the personal value of reading, and a means of sharing this with others. You may have fundraised, sought partners, become articulate in a pragmatic language to justify your intentions. And yet – as I recently found myself, sitting at the table for the very first 'Unwind with a Book' – the finest language for such a beginning is:

Hello everyone, my name's Casi. I'm here to read aloud with you.

The less that is prefaced the better. It is not reductive to say little, not careless to avoid ground rules, because 'not doing' here is a positive action; it is done in consciousness of the creative process of the group that will in time define its own end. Practitioners are encouraged to give permissions rather than rules: 'feel free to read along with me, to draw my attention, to share what you love or what puzzles you, to read aloud if you fancy it'. The aim is to build a shared practice within the group, not to enforce one that may limit its nature. It is for the same reason that context or biography is not necessary when sharing a piece of literature: in order to create a space in which you are in the process of creating thoughts, *action* – your good practice – must come *first*, even before the intention. It is the order of events in Walt Whitman's 'A Noiseless Patient Spider':

And you O my soul where you stand,
Surrounded, detached, in measureless oceans of space,
Ceaselessly musing, venturing, throwing, seeking
the spheres to connect them,
Till the bridge you will need be formed, till the ductile
anchor hold,

**Till the gossamer thread you fling catch somewhere,
O my soul.**

It is hard work, and can be frightening to find yourself in that 'measureless ocean.' 'Fling' is the perfect word in its hint at a desperate attempt into the unknown.

With no ground rules to follow, example is your best resource – the way in which you attend to the literature, attend to the group. I have been especially aware of this in the early days of this group: when new members join every week each session is potentially a first session. It is easy to forget how new shared reading can feel. As I was drawing the conversation back into the story during the first 'Unwind with a Book' session, one member stopped me: 'I really am enjoying this, but, can I ask you – I wonder if you could speed up your reading a bit? It's really quite slow, and my eyes keep on jumping ahead.' I have spent years in training courses encouraging people to slow the pace of their reading – it's a function of the attention that the literature demands of you. Here was the experience from the other end. It was good that she mentioned it – I had asked her to interrupt me after all – good that we discussed it as a group: 'Yes, it is slower than you'd read by yourself. I've found that it takes a while to settle into it'. It's even better now that I see, six weeks in, that she has met the pace herself, and uses the space offered to her by the group to visibly relax. There's a passage in E. F. Schumacher's *Small is Beautiful* – a new discovery for me, and wonderful – that says:

Our mind is not a blank, a *tabula rasa*. When we begin to think we can do so only because our mind is already filled with all sorts of ideas *with which* to think.

I feel that this must surely apply to action too, action as a form or forerunner of thought, in which the practice that we present in the group offers a new model with which to do reading. A different way to be with other people. In this sense every group that we run is 'training' as much as Read to Lead will ever be.

I'm thinking of Liz, another member of that very first session, who contributed throughout the discussion on the story – 'The

Twins' by Muriel Spark – but hardly said a word on the poem, 'The Beautiful Lie' by Sheenagh Pugh. In fact, hardly anyone spoke apart from me: 'I wonder what this is saying', 'This line, it's wonderful'... Despite what I know and tell others about initial reluctance to engage with poetry, the experience of it can still be flattening, especially when it's a piece that you love and want to do justice to. Next week, 'I Know Why the Caged Bird Sings' by Maya Angelou. More discussion this time, but Liz says nothing still. No Liz the week after: we read 'For a Five Year Old' by Fleur Adcock. The week following, Liz is back and we close the session with Jackie Kay's 'In My Country':

> **Walking by the waters**
> **down where an honest river**
> **shakes hands with the sea,**
> **a woman passed round me**
> **in a slow watchful circle,**
> **as if I were a superstition;**
>
> **or the worst dregs of her imagination,**
> **so when she finally spoke**
> **her words spliced into bars**
> **of an old wheel. A segment of air.**
> ***Where do you come from?***
> **'Here', I said. 'Here. These parts.'**

Liz looks up at me. She is not the first to speak, but she maintains eye contact and when her time comes she says: 'I wonder what that means – 'an honest river'? I've never heard a river described as 'honest' before'. I wonder if I would have spotted this as an important moment before now? When I first began running groups, I remember feeling anxious that people weren't making the connection between the writing and their own lives as explicitly as I hoped the model would encourage them to. That they weren't making the reading 'personal' enough. I was wrong to think that disclosure is the only mode of the personal. Liz's contribution here is personal reading: it is itself an honest thought, born in the combination of her experience and something new, unknown:

Not known, because not looked for
But heard, half-heard, in the stillness
Between two waves of the sea.

Liz, in her silence, had heard this, and her contribution that day was born, I believe, of those previous sessions in which she had said nothing, but in which she had observed an approach with which to think, to share, to do the reading.

Liz's contribution is a model to all of us running groups; it highlights the productiveness of a beginner's mind. Over time, it is almost inevitable that as a facilitator you will develop literary expertise, a natural by-product of being long in the company of books and paying personal attention to them. But partly it should work the other way around. It is in seeing a word as new – 'I've never heard a river described as honest before' – that the beginning of the creative process lies. A creative process and a useful one. Liz's thought helped other members of the group to express their own ideas, those mingling waters 'shaking hands'.

It is impossible to work at The Reader Organisation and be unaware of new beginnings. My group in Glasgow is only part of the development of our work in Scotland. We recently ran our first Welsh-language Read to Lead, a partnership led by Gwynedd Libraries bringing the Reading Revolution to north Wales. We are also in the process of designing a Register of Shared Reading Practitioners, exploring the means by which we can recognise quality practice in this field. It may not be surprising that T. S. Eliot was in our minds at the outset of this venture: 'We shall never cease from exploration.' It will not be easy to capture what is meant by quality practice, but insistence on quality has always been at the core of our work, that sense in

every phrase
And sentence that is right (where every word is at home,
Taking its place to support the others [...]
The complete consort dancing together).

As Barry in Salford said: 'That's spot on, that, spot on.'

POETRY

CHARLES WILKINSON

Double Vision

'...*bespangling every bough like stars*'
William Blake

The wallpaper was the worst,
stripping and repeating itself
in front of the eye, and later
the bed spinning round before
you vomited after that party
to honour the clever kid's
achievement. 'No wonder
he got a scholarship', you
said, 'he's got two heads.'
          But sober
morning's no joke: the
cap of lead that is your
skull, the thirst that woke
you up at dawn, those pale
stains of self that swim
across your sight.

Tomorrow must be
a new way of doubling riches
in the world, a day that puts
the glory back into the trees.
        Let's hope for exact
and loving modes of looking,
the tenderness of eye that
treats all objects with lightly
magic care, the fire–fuelled heart
recharging every cell; the stare
that has no pride, but sees
with wide and generous sight,
revising every instant into
lines of gold: the second vision.

YOUR REGULARS

THAT WHICH MAKES ME MAN
TEN YEARS OF GET INTO READING

Jane Davis

In my editorial in *The Reader* No.11, ten years ago, I wrote about reading 'Crossing The Bar' by Tennyson, with beginner readers of poetry:

In both groups, as I read the poem aloud, someone began to cry. I offered to stop, to change the poem, do something else. In both cases, the reader moved to tears said 'No, carry on. I want to read it.'

Those two groups were the first Get Into Reading groups, which I ran in community education centres in Birkenhead during the summer of 2002. My idea had been to try to take the kind of work I had been doing inside the University out into the wide world – that is, reading the great books of literature as if there were no body of literary criticism, as if my students and I were simply humans who had found a piece of writing on a bus and picked it up out of sheer interest. 'Great books out of the University' was my motto. When I looked back at it, I saw that that editorial began with a quotation which seemed to point at a terrible truth:

Poetry? Kill me now!
Bart Simpson

I don't know where I read that more people in the UK write poetry than read it, but I bet it's true, just as Bart's sentiment strikes home because you know you've felt it and so have lots of other people, especially young guys with skateboards, and, at the risk of sounding like someone who shares DNA with Michael Gove, the Secretary of State for Education here in the UK, I blame the way we are taught. On this point, actually, I probably go further than Mr Gove.

Say it is true that more people write poetry than read it. I find that supposition very heartening. It means that people feel a *need* for poetry, a need so powerful that they are willing to take pen to paper, put finger to keyboard, and to pull words up out of silence and into writing. That is a deeply creative act, however well or badly done.

Sadly, most such writing will *inevitably* be badly done, as most such writers do not think that their need for words will be helped by reading the great poetry of the past two thousand years. This is a waste. Writing is at least a craft and at best a great art. Anyone who does it (however badly) *is* doing it but, as with baking or oil painting, not everyone who does it achieves good results. Really doing it well, in all crafts, indeed in any creative endeavour, requires practice: learning from experience and from the experience of great masters is how people get better.

Most people who write poetry – in desperation, battered by fate, moved by the hugest experiences of human life – do not think of learning how to do it *better*. They just need some words *right now*. If the words help and excite them, then the writer may be led on to more writing, and in a positive feedback loop, they may begin to love writing so much that they will want to learn more about it. Loving doing something almost invariably leads to learning more about it, though the learning, being experiential, may be hard for us to recognise as learning. Great bikers love their bikes and know how to build, ride and fix them. The leather-clad, loud, biker convoy carries experts. Great bakers don't just manage to knock out a few flattish scones – they learn from the masters of the tradition and come up with delightful gooseberry savarins. Very good musicians go to even better musicians and learn from the masters. It's a kind of loving.

If bikers and bakers and bass players see the need to learn, why don't all those people who are moved to write poetry read poetry? The answer is that people have been immunised against poetry by bad education. I am using poet Les Murray's words here, from his poem 'The Instrument' , first published in *The Reader* No 2:

Who reads poetry? Not our intellectuals;
They want to control it...
...Not poor schoolkids
Furtively farting as they get immunized against it

Mass education may have worked when we were simply trying to make factory hands literate to read the safety instructions, or get pre-calculator clerks to know their multiplication tables off by heart, and it still works in a Zumba class (if everyone wants to be there), but we have failed to create a mass education which educates individuals for the hard sad task of being human. This is partly caused by the failure of people working in the Humanities to recognise the human value of their subjects. Among the many downsides of this is the two-thousand years' worth of literature mouldering unread in the stacks of closing libraries.

All of which is to say, when those readers were moved to tears by 'Crossing The Bar', I knew that I had stumbled into something important, though I had no idea what it was at the time. I knew it was to be my work, though I had no vision of The Reader Organisation becoming what it now is (an independent charity creating thousands of reading sessions every year, with sixty-three full-time staff and eighty volunteers, a social enterprise turning over £1.3m last year). I had no ambition except to get more reading of great literature to happen. I think I did understand explicitly what I had previously felt implicitly, that reading can give any of us access to feelings and thoughts we have, we suffer, but may not usefully *know*. Ten years on, with more than 330 Get Into Reading groups run every week by The Reader Organisation and hundreds more by people we have trained on our Read to Lead courses, I am pleased to report that the single most surprising thing about what happens in those reading groups is the utter delight arising from, and serious attention given to, poetry. People *love* reading poetry.

Last week I helped run a day of sessions for a group of people who have been doing our Read to Lead course. Several of the people on the course had been sent along by an NHS Drug and Alcohol Service. This day's work was as moving and powerful as anything I experienced in the early days of Get into Reading. As part of the course, our students were to select a poem of their own choice to read in a shared reading group with their colleagues – a chance to put what they had been learning into practice. All the chosen poems were impressive – for example, Thom Gunn's 'Human Condition' or Alexander Pope's 'Solitude' – and to read them in such company was a powerful experience. A few years ago some of these people would have been living lives dominated by drugs and/or alcohol, some of them homeless, others separated from people they love. These hard experiences are perhaps only extreme versions of all human lives, but because they are at the far edge of experience, they help bring into sharp focus the power of literature in a life. 'Now it is fog' begins the tremendous Thom Gunn poem, and I look around the table and wonder in which fogs we have all been walking.

> **Now it is fog. I walk**
> **Contained within my coat;**
> **No castle more cut off**
> **By reason of its moat:**
> **Only the sentry's cough,**
> **The mercenaries' talk.**
>
> **The street lamps, visible,**
> **Drop no light on the ground,**
> **But press beams painfully**
> **In a yard of fog around.**
> **I am condemned to be**
> **An individual.**

The poems addressed a complex and interconnected range of thoughts and feelings anyone might have about being a human, having a life to live; being with, or without, companionship.

And it took one of The Reader Organisation's young apprentices, newly out of foster-care and attempting to set up her life without the help of a family, to suggest that there was no coat, no castle, no moat. 'These are what you put on, to protect yourself, and yet they cut you off,' she said.

It seems almost miraculous to me that ten years on, I and so many colleagues should be outside of University, outside Continuing Education and outside the School of English where *The Reader* began, and that we should be reading, day in and day out, great literature with people who are not doing a course but simply trying to live their lives. That we should be reading with drug addicts and ex-alcoholics; with people in recovery and people in Care; those in deep physical or mental suffering; that we should be reading with psychiatrists and firefighters; with occupational therapists and mothers whose children have been taken away from them; with people who are profoundly deaf (we 'read aloud' through sign language) and with trainee teachers; with people at work and people living with dementia, and people in prison or on probation; that we should be developing community-readers' apprenticeships for care-leavers who may have little formal education and are about as far from a university English degree as it is possible to be. And that so many of these people should then want to learn how to pass on this reading revolution to others.

A supporter goes to visit a group in London and emails me that Lois, who was once a volunteer and who is now a staff member, is reading *Hamlet* with her group. A colleague writes me how she has loved reading and been hugely moved by Mrs Gaskell's *Wives and Daughters*. At my own group at a Drug and Alcohol service in Chester, we are about to start on Kipling's *Kim*. In prison, Al is finding that Ray Bradbury and George Saunders go down well, and at Forum Housing a housing officer is reading *Silas Marner* with her tenants' group. Not all groups will be reading literature of this quality all the time: we start from where we *can* start and we work our way into the greatest books, if that seems to be working for the people with whom we read. My colleague Angela Macmillan's wonderful *A Little, Aloud* anthologies contain all kinds of good things for adults and children to taste and try.

Brian Nellist's new poetry selection, *Minted: Practical Poems for Life* has 50 great things he wouldn't want a reader not to know.

Who'd have guessed when I walked, quaking with nerves, into that community education centre in Birkenhead, that all this would come about? That in Aarhus, Denmark, in Melbourne, Australia and in deepest Cornwall, and Easterhouse Glasgow, in Belfast's Hydebankwood Prison, people would be getting together to share reading every week, and to open together the wonderful storehouse of literature, and by reading personally, making the most powerful of inner and outer connections. As Thom Gunn writes:

> **I am my one touchstone.**
> **This is a test more hard**
> **Than any ever known.**
> **And thus I keep my guard**
> **On that which makes me man.**

We read aloud and test what we read against what we personally know. We share that testing conversation as much as we wish to share, and the rest we do in our inner privacy, and thus individually and collectively, getting into reading together, we remake our humanity, humanities. It is a kind of loving.

YOUR REGULARS

WHERE READING MEETS WRITING

Ian McMillan

I woke up early this morning, as I always do, 4.30, more of a concrete poem than a time. I lay there, looking at the ceiling, listening to a blackbird in the garden and an early car on the main road. I grabbed my little personal radio and listened for a while, quietly, on the headphones so as not to wake my wife. BBC Radio 5 Live told me all the news I needed to know, and so I turned to Radio 3 and Debussy told me more, much more, than I needed to know about anything. Maybe it was a bit of a mistake putting the Debussy on because he soured the day for words. Somehow this piano music felt more profound, more comforting, than the sports news on 5 Live even though I knew in my wordy heart that it wasn't.

Words are me, as the name of that Toy Shop almost says. Years ago, when I worked as a Literature Development Worker in Doncaster, my first task was to sack that word 'literature' and replace it with the more inclusive word 'words'. I became Words Worker because I knew that a lot of the people we worked with would run a mile from the idea of Literature but they knew how to use words, even if they weren't so good at writing them down or reading them out if they managed to write them down.

I get up. I go downstairs. I go out for my early morning stroll and, instead of listening to a wordy podcast as I often do on my walk, I listen to the world instead, a world that seems to get by without words. And in particular the written word; somehow, when I'm in this mood, the spoken or sung word feels okay, feels legitimate, but the written word feels like plastic surgery or triple glazing; unnecessary, over the top. Feels to me that this is going to be one of those days when I have to re-teach myself to read, re-acquaint myself with the joy of reading.

So I'll start with car number plates, For Sale signs on a couple of houses down Garden Street, names on the backs of white vans. I'll get home and have my breakfast, reading the side of the cereal packet, gradually warming up to the idea of those shapes that make letters, that make words.

Now I'll read something that's mainly pictures, just to fool myself back into the word-place. How's this: *Groundtastic*. The new issue came yesterday and I've not had time to look at it yet. *Groundtastic* is a wonderful quarterly magazine devoted to non-league football grounds and I think I've written about it before in *The Reader*, but you can never get too much *Groundtastic* or 'the pornography of corrugated iron sheds' as my wife calls it. Each issue is full of photographs of football stands, and, as ever, the photographs lead me to the written word.

So here's an image of one of the two identical new stands at Team Solent's ground, and here's a paragraph that teeters between information and poetry: 'Test Park unveiled a pair of surprisingly stylish stands. Each featuring five rows of well-raked seating, the gleaming metal tiers and similarly shiny red seats are enclosed by roofs that curve round in one continuous sweep.' And they do: have a look at the picture. I'm enjoying this reading. Written words are coming back to me. There's an elegiac piece about the old Sector Lane ground at Axminster Town, which has just had its last season: 'In the event, the last ever first team match at Sector Lane, an SWPL Division One East fixture on 24th March 2012, saw the visitors Crediton United cruise to an

8-2 win. Watched by just 68 spectators, it was a low key and rather ignominious end to 91 years of football at the venue.'

Now it's time to try some more creative writing. I've just got a copy of an old Robert Benchley book and, like the *Groundtastic*, I've not had time to read it yet. Robert Benchley was an American humourist of the kind I like, writing gorgeous sentences for magazines like *The New Yorker*. He was in the James Thurber and S. J. Perelman mould, although less sentimental than the former and not as wordy as the latter. Let me open the book at random and read, from a fantastic satirical piece called 'The Social Life of the Newt': 'Since that time I have practically lived amongst newts, jotting down observations, making lantern-slides, watching them in their work and in their play (and you may rest assured that the little rogues have their play – as who does not?) until, from much lying in a research posture on my stomach, over the inclosure in which they were confined, I found myself developing what I feared may be the rudimentary creepers. And so, late this Autumn, I stood erect and walked into my house, where I immediately set about the compilation of the notes I had made.' I'm grinning like a fool as I read this. The 'rudimentary creepers'! Fantastic! The idea of calling newts 'little rogues': brilliant. Now I'm beginning to love reading again, beginning to love the places it can take me.

I get an email from my daughter who's on holiday in France with her son, my grandson, Thomas. She's sent a picture: ah, there he is, on the campsite, reading his *Detective's Handbook*. Always reading.

Now it's time for a bit of the hard stuff after the *amuse-bouche* and the first course. Time for some Peter Larkin. Larkin is one of my favourite poets, writing a kind of deep nature or radical landscape poetry that makes me gasp. When I read Peter Larkin I feel that I'm reading completely: I'm fully involved in the history of language and the possible futures it might have, I'm taking my time and letting lines soak into me, I'm trying to make myself aware of a whole poetic tradition as I take in the words, and I'm helping to create the meaning, which is, of course, where reading meets writing. That's me for the day: sinking into Peter Larkin, back in love with reading:

'Unblown offered recorded, slightened at will, between the skinny re-entry bays of the wood. The intrusion of a breach into its own healing space, a sill of reserve. So blunted among own foreclosure, it stains the gift of this place, patrolling the rounds of true burden beyond offer.'

Let me read that again. And again. And again.

Groundtastic: www.groundtastic.co.uk

The Benchley Roundup by Robert Benchley. My edition was published in 1954 by Harper & Row, and I got it from Abe Books.

Lessways Least Scarce Among by Peter Larkin published by Shearsman www.shearsman.com

YOUR REGULARS

Brian Nellist

Q *The Reader* remains rather reserved about popular culture, nothing about graphic books or even television and cinema. Yet we all know that as writers supplying a market Shakespeare and Dickens, for example, would today be producing the best soap operas ever. Never mention money?

A Yes, I know; Aristotle would be Mr Wikipedia and Homer permanently at number one in the charts. But no; you can't take figures out of their complex historical situations and simply drop them into appropriate contemporary slots without falling into pure fantasy. The danger of the term 'popular culture' lies in making the various modes of expression subject to a kind of class war whereas Shakespeare and Dickens, oh yes, influenced by all sorts of popular genres and activities, wrote, wrote my questioner, for the sovereign, peers of the realm, merchants, apprentices, prostitutes and sturdy rogues, anyone who could read or would listen. So the money came in but there is no internal or external evidence to demonstrate that that was the efficient cause for the way they wrote rather than the result of their success. Such writers make their own 'market' instead of 'supplying' an existent demand and still do. Your use of 'today' implies that the dramatist and the novelist are in some way 'out of date'. If *Eastenders* is for now then so are Shakespeare and Dickens, and for tomorrow and the day after that, world without end.

More worryingly, you imply that even the play and the novel themselves are out of date and have been displaced not by new verbal modes but by the visual, as though with the invention of flight, trains and ships have become unnecessary. The title of our magazine is not a metaphor for gazing at the stars or interpreting someone's features. We mean it literally (literally); words are still the means by which we affect each other and the written word, the considered utterance, the discovery by a writer in that very act of where he or she stands, remains fundamental to who we are, to the very structure of the mind, and I say that, who find it very difficult and have never done much writing in fact. What is it that words offer that's different from visual media?

When I was eleven, I was taken to see David Lean's wonderful film of *Great Expectations* and was bowled over by the opening sequence, of course. For weeks I was haunted by that threatening sound of wind in the great trees, the isolation of the church, the emptiness of the landscape beyond and Finlay Currie, the desperate ogre almost materialised by the boy Pip's fears. But the text does something different. That hostile country is home; 'Ours was the marsh country'. But who are 'we'? All that's been mentioned yet are the graves of his parents and of five 'little' graves, though of course they belong to his older brothers. In a novel whose title indicates hopes and ambitions how powerful are those origins going to be, an escape from a landscape of death? An answer is maybe suggested when Magwitch springs on him, though we're told about it before that happens, 'My first most vivid and broad impression of the identity of things'. This is the voice of the disillusioned older Pip but to him now remembering it's as though, behind all his dreams about Miss Havisham's generosity, his destiny with Estella and his prosperity as apprentice blacksmith turned gentleman, there was always buried in his mind that other image of the 'identity of things', not home but the world turned upside down, the fear of the bullied orphan that things could be even worse. I'm still not as moved by that as I was instantly by Lean's opening images but it makes me reflect, gives me something to think with and connects me with the rest of the novel. Lean takes you to a memorable place but Dickens takes you into your own life. Dickens wouldn't have been David Lean but, even today, the novelist himself.

The relationship between the 'popular' and 'art' modes, for want of a better pair of terms, has always been in two directions.

If Wordsworth draws on the street ballad then ballads themselves used elements from earlier courtly writing. If you praise soap opera as one innovative popular form, its use of multiple story lines and cunningly inter-cut scenes draws on theatrical traditions manifest in Shakespeare's histories, for example, and *Henry IV* could be what you call 'the best soap opera ever'. No one in it is wholly admirable except from some special point of view. The king fighting rebels is himself a rebel and his guilt would seek atonement by going to Jerusalem, walked by;

those blessed feet
Which fourteen hundred years ago were nail'd
For our advantage on the bitter cross.

Yet he is to die at the end of Part 2 only in the Jerusalem Chamber at Westminster leaving his blood-soaked land as legacy to his son. And that son seeks release from the family guilt through dangerous games with Falstaff, boon companion set up for betrayal by Hal from the start. But then the apparently good-hearted, clever, convivial fat knight beyond it all reduces the issues to self-preservation, coldly ready to turn underlings into battle-fodder and dismiss his own friends, Peto, Bardolph, Poins, if only he can stay in favour. The charisma and energy of the chief soldier of the rebels, Hotspur, produces however, a rhetoric:

By heaven methinks it were an easy leap
To pluck bright honour from the pale-fac'd moon

where only his enthusiasm and sincerity save it from absurdity. The relation between the scenes is more complex, the design, the depth, the authority of the language is of course beyond what you'll find even in exceptionally gifted good soap opera but the kinship, if you'll accept it, also throws up another difference which is critical. The three scenes of Act 1 would take say three-quarters of an hour to act whereas scenes on television last two or three minutes. So much more is going on in the play that the time is needed for our minds to walk through the issues, the situations, the relationships. Try to imagine what it would be like to extend a single scene to that length in a TV narrative and you'll see which medium has to hurry on in order to avoid tedium.

POETRY

PAT FARRINGTON

Figures on a landscape

Dot of red for a cap,
scumble of white
for a ragged shirt,
quick downstroke
in matted grey,
not close enough
to see the muscles
necessary for survival;
placed there for scale
in sweeps of ancient landscape,
figures added at the very end.

So lightly painted on the canvas,
these transient rustics hardly touch
the surface of the earth,
their burial place.

BOOKS ABOUT...

SINGLE WOMEN

Angela Macmillan

Recently I realised I had been reading, more by accident than design, good strong novels about the lives of single women. They have not necessarily made for cheerful reading but they have all been deeply involving. When I looked for novels depicting the single status as happy and fulfilling, which it often is, I ran into difficulty: Miss Marple, and Miss Read perhaps, even Miss Garnett or Miss Pettigrew. I will have to go back to that search, but for now here are five books which, though often sad, tell of love, courage, duty and fortitude and which thoughtfully explore the obscure shape of personal feeling in the secret places of women's lives.

Elizabeth Taylor, *A Wreath of Roses*, 1949
ISBN-13: 978-1844087129

During an intensely hot summer, just after the Second World War, Camilla Hill, a school secretary, arrives at an English village to holiday as usual with her great friend Liz and Liz's former governess, now an artist, Frances. But things have changed. Liz has married and has a new baby and Frances seems suddenly old and preoccupied. Feeling excluded, Camilla is drawn into a relationship with a man, despite every instinct warning her against him. For me, this is the *finest* of Elizabeth Taylor's fine novels. The depth and reality of the relationship between the three women in all its familiarity and difference is quite superb. She is brilliant at the ways in which we knowingly deceive ourselves and creates an atmosphere of voluptuous summer that is at once beguiling and chilling.

Edith Wharton, *The Old Maid*, 1924
ISBN-13: 978-0486476858

New York society in the 1850s was stiff with rules and conventions at a time when old families despised new money. However, this book is much more than just a portrait of an age. The price of a brief, passionate affair for Charlotte is her illegitimate daughter whom she must give into the care of her widowed cousin, Delia, to bring up as her own. The highly charged emotional struggle between and within the two women: passion, jealousy and the conflicting pressures of maternal love, lie like 'dark destinies coiled under the safe surface of life'. The film of the book starred Bette Davis as Charlotte. A terrific performance, but not a lot to do with Edith Wharton's story.

Margaret Laurence, *Rachel, Rachel*
(also known as *A Jest of God*), 1966
ISBN-13: 978-0226469522

Following the death of her father, Rachel gives up any possibility of an independent life and returns to a small town in Canada to teach in grade school and look after her peevish, self-centred mother whom she resents but loves. Shockingly, this book is out of print now. Margaret Laurence deserves and needs to be better known. Her portrait of Rachel, hungry of mind and body, unbearably lonely but ultimately strong is real and true.

Anne Brontë, *Agnes Grey***, 1847**
ISBN-13: 978-1853262166

A short novel written from first-hand experience of life as a governess. It is her first novel and not as great as the *Tenant of Wildfell Hall* but it is powerful in its depiction of a woman leaving the loving closeness of home to be treated as less than nothing by her employers and the children whom she teaches. The cruelty and deprivation make for difficult reading but Anne often writes with an understated and quietly endearing humour:

> **The following day was as fine as the preceding one. Soon after breakfast Miss Matilda, having galloped and blundered through a few unprofitable lessons, and vengefully thumped the piano for an hour, in a terrible humour with both me and it, because her mama would not give her a holiday, had betaken herself to her favourite place of resort, the yards, the stables and the dog-kennels.**

F. M. Mayor, *The Rector's Daughter***, 1924**
ISBN-13: 978-0860689119

Since being chosen by Susan Hill as her 'Neglected Classic' on BBC Radio 4's *Open Book*, this novel has been enjoying some high recommendations on the literary blogosphere – deservedly so. Here is another book about the subordinate and lonely lives of women who care for others at the cost of self-fulfilment. But if you haven't come across it, please read it. For in Mary Jocelyn, Flora Mayor presents us with a real woman in all her hopes and fears, her low self-esteem and her high sense of duty and capacity to love. And you will care about her.

Edited by
ANGELA MACMILLAN

A Little,
ALOUD
for children

An anthology of poems and stories
to share aloud

Financial Times
Book of the Year
for Children

'An absolutely
impeccable
anthology'

£9.99 RRP

Or £5.99 (+ p&p)
from www.
thereader.org.uk

With a foreword by
MICHAEL MORPURGO

A LITTLE *MORE* ALOUD

FROM ELIZABETH GASKELL'S *CRANFORD*

Chosen by Angela Macmillan

One of the reasons that *Cranford* is such a joy is the seamless blending of the comic and the serious. This gently funny and moving moment is typical. Mary Smith is staying in Cranford with Miss Matty who was her mother's friend.

Chapter 5. Old Letters

I have often noticed that almost every one has his own individual small economies – careful habits of saving fractions of pennies in some one peculiar direction – any disturbance of which annoys him more than spending shillings or pounds on some real extravagance. An old gentleman of my acquaintance, who took the intelligence of the failure of a Joint-Stock Bank, in which some of his money was invested, with stoical mildness, worried his family all through a long summer's day because one of them had torn (instead of cutting) out the written leaves of his now useless bank-book; of course, the corresponding pages at the other end came out as well, and this little unnecessary waste of paper (his private economy) chafed him more than all the loss of his money. Envelopes fretted his soul terribly when they first came in; the only way in which he could reconcile himself to such waste of his cherished article was by patiently turning inside out all that were sent to him, and so making them serve again. Even now, though tamed by age, I see him casting wistful glances at his daughters when they send a whole inside of a half-sheet of note paper, with the three lines of acceptance to an invitation, written on only one of the sides. I am not above owning that I have this human weakness myself. String is my foible. My pockets get full of little hanks of it, picked up and twisted together, ready for uses that never come. I am seriously annoyed if any one cuts the string of a parcel instead of patiently and faithfully undoing it fold by fold. How people can bring themselves to use india-rubber rings, which are a sort of deification of string, as lightly as they do, I cannot imagine. To me an india-rubber ring is a precious treasure. I have one which is not new – one that I picked up off the floor nearly six years ago. I have really tried to use it, but my heart failed me, and I could not commit the extravagance.

Small pieces of butter grieve others. They cannot attend to conversation because of the annoyance occasioned by the habit which some people have of invariably taking more butter than they want. Have you not seen the anxious look (almost mesmeric) which such persons fix on the article? They would feel it a relief if they might bury it out of their sight by popping it into their own mouths and swallowing it down; and they are really made happy if the person on whose plate it lies unused suddenly breaks off a piece of toast (which he does not want at all) and eats up his butter. They think that this is not waste.

Now Miss Matty Jenkyns was chary of candles. We had many devices to use as few as possible. In the winter afternoons she would sit knitting for two or three hours – she could do this in the dark, or by firelight – and when I asked if I might not ring for candles to finish stitching my wristbands, she told me to 'keep blind man's holiday'. They were usually brought in with tea; but we only burnt one at a time. As we lived in constant preparation for a friend who might come in any evening (but who never did), it required some contrivance to keep our two candles of the same length, ready to be lighted, and to look as if we burnt two always. The candles took it in turns; and, whatever we might be talking about or doing, Miss Matty's eyes were habitually fixed upon the candle, ready to jump up and extinguish it and to light the other before they had become too uneven in length to be restored to equality in the course of the evening.

One night, I remember this candle economy particularly annoyed me. I had been very much tired of my compulsory 'blind man's holiday', especially as Miss Matty had fallen asleep, and I did not like to stir the fire and run the risk of awakening her; so I could not even sit on the rug, and scorch myself with sewing by firelight, according to my usual custom. I fancied Miss Matty must be dreaming of her early life; for she spoke one or two words in her uneasy sleep bearing reference to persons who were dead long before. When Martha brought in the lighted candle and tea, Miss Matty started into wakefulness, with a strange, bewildered look around, as if we were not the people she expected to see about her. There was a little sad expression that shadowed her face as she recognised me; but immediately afterwards she tried to give me her usual smile. All through tea-time her talk ran upon the days of her childhood and youth. Perhaps this reminded her of the desirableness of looking over all the old family letters, and destroying such as ought not to be allowed to fall into the hands of strangers; for she had often spoken of the necessity of this task, but had always shrunk from it, with a timid dread of something painful. To-night, however, she rose up after tea and went for them – in the dark; for she piqued herself on the precise neatness of all her chamber arrangements, and used to look uneasily at me when I lighted a bed-candle to go to another room for anything. When she returned there was a faint, pleasant smell of Tonquin beans in the room. I had always noticed this scent about any of the things which had belonged to her mother; and many of the letters were addressed to her – yellow bundles of love-letters, sixty or seventy years old.

Miss Matty undid the packet with a sigh; but she stifled it directly, as if it were hardly right to regret the flight of time, or of life either. We agreed to look them over separately, each taking a different letter out of the same bundle and describing its contents to the other before destroying it. I never knew what sad work the reading of old-letters was before that evening, though I could hardly tell why. The letters were as happy as letters could be – at least those early letters were. There was in them a vivid and intense sense of the present time, which seemed so strong and full, as if it could never pass away, and as if the warm, living hearts that so expressed themselves could never die, and be as nothing to the sunny earth. I should have felt less melancholy, I believe, if the letters had been more so. I saw the tears stealing down the well-worn furrows of Miss Matty's cheeks, and her spectacles often wanted wiping. I trusted at last that she would light the other candle, for my own eyes were rather dim, and I wanted more light to see the pale, faded ink; but no, even through her tears, she saw and remembered her little economical ways.

READERS CONNECT

WITH
VINTAGE CLASSICS

ELIZABETH BOWEN
THE HEAT OF THE DAY

It's an interesting book this time, likely to divide opinion. Some will be exasperated by Bowen's diction – those impossible long sentences. Others will be intrigued by her characters who struggle

to know (or not to know) themselves under wartime conditions and the general sense that 'careless talk costs lives'.

I have to say that *The Heat of the Day* is a curious reading experience. Take for instance the discrepancy between the inside and the outside of things. There are pages of description, densely over-doing it, and then you have the elliptical conversations, which drive the action, in which you struggle to catch at straws of sense. Is Stella's lover a spy? What of the mysterious Cousin Francis? Can her son Roderick break free of the unspeaking past? Counter-agent Harrison is not quite at the heart of the book and yet he holds the key to its tone. Stella talks to him during a fall of rain:

> **'Have you far to go?'**
> **'Depends where I go to next'**
> **'Where exactly do you live? I have no idea.'**
> **'There are always two or three places where I can turn in.'**
> **'But for instance, where do you keep your razor?'**
> **'I have two or three razors,' he said in an absent tone.**
> **That, of course, was the core of their absolute inhumanity together... By the rules of fiction, with which life to be credible must comply, he was as a character 'impossible' – each time they met, for instance, he showed no shred or trace of having been continuous since they last met.**

Lynne Hatwell (dovegreyreader) is a Devon-based community nurse

Can anyone create a sense of place and populate it with such depth of character and event as Elizabeth Bowen? This reads like one of those important books that give voice to a moment in time – the unseen threats of wartime London in the hands of a writer who knew of them. Read Bowen's superlative prose slowly and deliberately and hear a people, a city and a nation under threat.
* * * *

Mette Steenberg is the founder/director of Laeseforeningen (The Reading Society) in Denmark

If 'intelligent' means lengthy descriptions and cartoon-like depictions of character alongside clichés and spelled-out 'wisdom', then this noir might be, as the *Los Angeles Times*, claims 'the most intelligent noir ever written'. It offers nothing to the intellect. So if you are not a noir aficionado, don't bother. Here is nothing but style. Donald Duck is a less of a caricature and deeper in his wisdom.

0

Drummond Moir, once of Edinburgh, works for a London-based publisher

I was expecting a noir/spy story, but it felt like a confused cross between this and family drama. The descriptions of wartime London, though, are fantastic – the city's exhausted populace are haunted by the fallen, 'uncounted and unknown'; 'wariness had driven away poetry: from hesitating to feel came the moment when you no longer could.' Chilling.
*

STAR RATINGS

***** one of the best books I've read
**** one of the best I've read this year
*** highly recommended

** worth reading
* not for me but worth trying
0 don't bother

REVIEWS

'ANNOUNCEMENTS OF THE NATURAL'

Kathleen Jamie, *Sightlines*

Sort Of Books, 2012, £8.99

ISBN 9-780956-308665

Julie-ann Rowell

athleen Jamie's *Sightlines* comprises fourteen essays for 'the island-goers'. I understand the sentiment. These inspiring nature essays are very much about looking, seeing, which is not as easy as it sounds. Goethe said, 'the hardest thing to see is what is in front of your eyes,' and Benoît Mandelbrot thought the eye 'the most important instrument of thought'. For nature observation how to look is crucial, and Jamie certainly has the 'eye', she observes acutely and can transcribe her observations fluidly, and straightforwardly, with the occasional leaping simile. Her imagery is memorable – 'if we could taste the green aurora it would fizz on the tongue and taste like crème de menthe'. I enjoy her vocabulary, the 'screaking terns' and 'gurly sea'. It helps to conjure the wildness of the places we are taken to: St Kilda, Rona, Shetland, an icy fjord off Greenland, where at times the cold and the wind is unbearable. But remoteness can be found in many locations, including a cave in Spain, filled with prehistoric art. The cave interior is like being in 'a hall of similes'. Also, the inner world of bodies, our pathologies, which she explores with Professor Frank Carey at Ninewells Hospital in Dundee; ironically she has to physically travel downwards in the hospital's corridors, as in La Cueva, to see intimately, a section of a human colon, a magnification of the liver.

Jamie reminds us of the gift of that glimpse we can catch into nature, the sighting of a pod of killer whales, a storm petrel, a magpie moth. How brief and yet indelible such encounters can prove to be. I remember my first (land) sighting of a right whale. It is a clear, sharp memory where so many other memories are diluted and scattered.

One of the essays I enjoyed the most was 'The Gannetry', where a colony of birds is brilliantly evoked, this mess of noisy, fractious, libidinous life set on one intent only, to breed, the urge overpowering, as they gather in the full sun, 'lured to their traditional cliffs and stacks by a siren song'.

She is not sentimental about what she discovers and yet there is at times a hint of reverence. But there is honest and pertinent observation about the cycle of nature: 'Populations expand, then crash. Mysterious things happen – catastrophic things sometimes, on the island, everywhere.' It happened to the human population of the remote island of Rona, who were wiped out, and no one knows quite how. Now the leach's petrel, described in the essay 'On Rona', are diminishing for reasons unknown, but even with all this Jamie hopes the island may be 'pressed into service again' in the 'unimaginable' future.

She has a particular fascination with whales and whalebones. Our terrible history cannot be avoided here. One essay 'The Hvalsalen' takes us into the Hvalsalen, a hall of whalebone in the Bergen Natural History Museum, 'not just the jaws – the entire skeletons, the ribcages, the great fans of scapulas and fin-bones, at the sides, the long receding trains of the spines'. These old brown bones are being conserved by a team of specialists, and it is as if they are coming alive again. The effect of the Hvalsalen is 'dreamlike'. The essay makes me want to see for myself.

She explores the fashion of displaying whale jawbones in-land, as arches, and the vertebrae held aloft at the Brough of Birsay on Orkney, a place I have visited for over twenty years. The vertebrae resembles, from a distance, a giant bird about to take flight, but is in its essence pelagic, and those of us who are, or who want to be, 'island-goers' desire to speak that language.

Jamie finishes her dynamic, vivid book of essays with the wind, always the wind – the residents of the Orkney Islands could say a thing about that.

REVIEWS

PROUST, PUNK ROCK AND PICALILLI

Ian McMillan, *This Lake Used to be Frozen: Lamps*
Smith / Doorstop books; Shellied, 2011
ISBN 978-1906613402

Brian Nellist

He sits on the six o'clock train from Newcastle to King's Cross opposite an executive lady tearing up CVs. Did it happen? Was it imagined? These are poems that like surrealist verse dissolve the customary frontiers between internal and external. What's solid in the poem is a free-floating, detached staple, glinting in the sun, catching the eye repeatedly. The fragments from other people's lives:

> **'My experience includes:**
> **Inventing new names for tree-trunks &**
> **eating wheelbarrows'**

in their mixture of the superfluous and the absurd enclose a serious sense of the impossibility of summarising lives for the marketplace of employment. Even the title is another scrap entering the mind from a floating voice, 'Did You Ask for a Decaf off that Other Lady?' The entirely ordinary becomes bizarre escaping from its context in someone's thirst or travelling boredom. Sorry, Ian! Here I am subjecting these light, airy, funny, inventive, unpredictable lines to the usual torpid drag of lit crit.

A lot of surrealist poetry of the thirties strikes me as also inventive but ever so slightly pretentious and Freudian chilly whereas Mr McMillan's verse has the warmth and glow of someone living in 'one familiar place', Barnsley. Its authenticity is caught in its voices, his father's or 'Norman Stopped Me on the Street' or a collier, as in 'Pitman Speyks':

> **Nowt else suits. Desk job, security, men**
> **In a daft hat. No chance.**

Inevitability, in a mining town, has to be turned into choice. That's from a mining sequence, 'Drift', unsentimental but interior to the pain and gruff togetherness of a nearly-vanished industry. The accuracy and oddity of detail comes from the importance of walking the streets and hills, the subject of another series of poems. They used to say it was the farmer's boot made the hills fertile but a poet also has to see and hear in the sort of detail that only a foot-patrol can achieve, not one of those fancy trails recommended by the Sunday supplements but beating the bounds of the parish, as it were. Repetition, seeing the same familiar spots over and over again through the years is to walk through memory into a history:

> **Top Field to Bottom Club, Snape Hill down past the**
> **Dancing School,**
> **Route I took as a child to the Valley, once dropped a**
> **threepenny bit**
> **In the postbox by the butcher's gone now, then**
> **postbox gone now.**
>
> (Walk 1)

The layering of experience turns memory into a palimpsest, 'I remember remembering, and the remembering remembers...'

What this book recollects even more often than the landscape, its seasons and its accidents, is those human voices through passing talk, friends in the street, family members. Two conversations at once from Roy and John, cut across each other, one about Radio Sheffield, the other about a holiday on Skye, and details of midges and the newish road bridge intersect information about the changing schedules. You'll all recognise the situation as something we relegate to a normal state of confusion but it becomes here liberated into freshness, the ordinary estranged. No wonder it's introduced by the unnervingly self-conscious lines:

Always for me, the struggle
Between populism and
Linguistically interesting work.

No need to worry; it is this multiple writing of memory and the moment, the accidental and the familiar, repetition, and the unique which produces the poetry. The effect is not of 'struggle' but of the felicitous and, occasionally, the alarming. It's a mixture of Proust, punk rock and piccalilli and long may it thrive.

BUCK'S QUIZ

'SITTING AT MY PIANO, THE OTHER DAY...'

Angela Macmillan

1. Who sends a large sized square pianoforte to Jane Fairfax?
2. Who sent a timid young girl a piano with 'cunning brackets to hold candles and the nice green silk, puckered up, with a gold rose in the middle'?
3. Who admitted to playing the piano, 'a little' and was told to take a candle, go to the library and play a tune'?
4. In his longing for which *particular* evenings does the poet see 'a child sitting under the piano, in the boom of the tinkling strings'?
5. 'The very first chords which Mademoiselle Reisz struck upon the piano sent a keen tremor down Mrs Pontellier's spinal column'. What is the title of the book?
6. In 1930s California, which mother waits on tables and eventually opens a chicken restaurant in order to pay for piano lessons for her awful daughter Veda?
7. Who said, 'Please don't shoot the pianist. He is doing his best'?
8. A German officer saved the life of which Jewish pianist when he brought food to the Warsaw Ghetto where the pianist was hiding?
9. In 1886 an Englishman is asked by The War Office to travel to the jungles of Burma to tune a rare piano. What is his name?
10. In which novel does the heroine enter the drawing room to find Madame Merle 'playing something of Schubert's... and she touched the piano with a discretion of her own. It showed skill, it showed feeling'?

THE READER CROSSWORD

Cassandra

ACROSS

9. Traditionally they take seventy years to construct fifty-one iron bridges (9)
10. Decree cited translation (5)
11. Helena I've found to be innocent at heart (5)
*12 and 19. Apologist for Richard in 18 and 2 down (9,3)
13. Hustles about to reveal investigators (7)
14. Nothing in real disposition of flight controller (7)
17. Initially new orthopaedic doctor eases sore joints (5)
* 19. See 12 across
* 20. See 1 down
21. Apple offers backhander following cocktail (7)
22. Battle for project space (7)
24. Simplistic rendering of catechism (9)
26. Stuck in a car jam, a fiasco for criminal organisation (5)
28. You generally need three of this item to celebrate (5)
* 29 and 23 down. Voting rights leading to intrigue and title (9, 6)

* Clues with an asterisk have a common theme

DOWN

*1 and 20 across. A local area network permit required for 12's one of 13 (4,5)
* 2. See 18 down
3. Fire repellent is possible cause of lung disease (10)
4. Music makers discovered in the middle of urban jostle (6)
5. A toy steamship is helpful in restoring state of equilibrium (8)
6. Aid for maid? (4)
7. Combination of motorway and first class rail return can cause a rash (8)
8. Pen a note describing eyesore (4)
13. 12 has them singing (5)
15. Marriage brings this to any issue (10)
16. Was musical script significant? (5)
* 18 and 2 down. Title of 12's description of truth (8,2,4)
19. Court official makes extra payment to workforce (8)
22. Two men combine to make one predator (6)
*23. See 29 across
24. Dry time for religious group (4)
25. Notice stain (4)
27. Where gentlemen in England find themselves, according to Harry (4)

PRIZES

The winner of the Crossword (plucked in time-honoured tradition from a hat) will receive a book prize courtesy of Vintage Classics, and the same to the winner of the fiendishly difficult Buck's Quiz.

Congratulations to Tony Anstey (Buck's Quiz), and to both Pam Nixon and Steve Bowkett (Crossword).

Please send your solutions (marked Cassandra Crossword or Buck's Quiz) to The Reader Organisation, The Friary Centre, Bute Street, Liverpool, L5 3LA. The deadline for answers is 5 October 2012.

ANSWERS

CASSANDRA CROSSWORD NO. 38

Across
1. Ablest 4. Lambda 9. View 10. Wonderland 11. Sensei 12. Cheshire 13. Snufflers 15. Hare 16. Quod 17. Intersect 21. Referees 22. Lemurs 24. Unsporting 25. Room 26. Fetish 27. Lethal

Down
1. Alice 2. Lewis 3. Sawmill 5. Aretes 6. Bulkheads 7. Aintree 8. Anachronistic 14. Flowerpot 16. Queen of 18. Eclogue 19. Carroll 20. Hearts 23. March

BUCK'S QUIZ NO. 46

1. Tiny Tim, *A Christmas Carol* 2. Mr Smallweed, *Bleak House* 3. Wilkins Micawber, *David Copperfield* 4. Mr Gradgrind, *Hard Times* 5. Uriah Heep, *David Copperfield* 6. Mr Jarndyce, *Bleak House* 7. Mrs Gummidge, *David Copperfield* 8. Mrs Gamp, *Martin Chuzzlewit* 9. The gentleman in the small-clothes, *Nicholas Nickleby* 10. Grip the raven, *Barnaby Rudge* 11. Mr Bumble, *Oliver Twist* 12. Lady Deadlock, *Bleak House* 13. Miss Pross, *A Tale of Two Cities* 14. Paul Dombey, *Dombey and Son* 15. Joe Gargery, *Great Expectations*

ESSAY

MOON, MOONSHINE, MOONING ETC

Alan Wall

Before 1610 nobody could say moon and signify any celestial body but the one circling our terrestrial home. Then Galileo fashioned his telescope, saw the moons of Jupiter, and published *Sidereus Nuncius*. Now there were other moons, though the new usage took a while to catch on. It's only in the latter half of the seventeenth century that the Philosophical Transactions of the Royal Society register the word as applying to anything other than the one nearest ourselves.

Some of the earliest prototypes of science fiction feature a trip to the moon, including Kepler's *Somnium* and H. G. Wells' novel of 1901. And the very first years of cinema show us the man in the moon having a rocket plunge into his face; this is one of the earliest of cinematic effects, courtesy of Méliès in 1902. We have always had a close relationship with our immediate neighbour in space. Our tides are regulated by its motions, and one half of the human species enjoys a biological rhythm as potent as the tides. Moon and month go back to the earliest traces of our languages: mens, mensuration, menstruation. Out of the Old English *mona* comes both moon and month. We first recorded time and season by reference to the moon, its phases and its faces. Yeats was still calculating civilizational progress or regress according to its revelations and occlusions in *A Vision*. And one way to flatter Queen Elizabeth the First was by talking about her in association with goddesses connected with the moon: Diana and Cynthia. For the poet it has always been seen to be complicit with the imagination. Curious transformations and witchy goings-on occur frequently enough in Shakespeare in the moonlight. But our little circling neighbour is still there as a potent force, both symbol and emblem, in Wallace Stevens and Sylvia Plath. For the latter the moon is nun, necromancer, and shaven-headed victim all in one, seen above the yew trees in the graveyard. And the quality of light, in contrast to sunlight, registers as unearthly. Too much influence from this body means one might be moonstruck, or even emerge as some kind of monstrous creature, a mooncalf perhaps. In Johnson's Dictionary, alongside the freak that is a mooncalf, we have a moonling, a simpleton who might well have been moonstruck.

If we wish to sound more scientific, we do what we usually do, upping the lexical ante by going Latin: here we might observe a lunatic. In employing that usage we announce that this is not merely abuse, but genuine diagnosis, aetiology even. *Loonie* merely indicates a temporary irritation with someone's tomfoolery. There are milder versions of the influence to be detected, of course. One might simply be mooning about. And then there's moonshine. Originally a description of the distinctiveness of the celestial body's reflected light, and often contrasted in the seventeenth century with earthshine, whose reciprocal effect can be seen on the moon's surface at night, it came to be employed in the eighteenth century as a designation for illegal liquor. This was originally an American usage, and it probably arose from the fact that those avoiding state taxes imposed on booze by manufacturing their own, had a tendency to do their distilling at night. Perhaps in allusion to the befuddling of the wits which hard liquor (whether legal or not) tends to induce, moonshine then came to mean nonsense, or wishful thinking. David Attenborough records how he tried to raise the subject of continental drift with his lecturer at Oxford in the 1940s, and was told that the idea, in the absence of any concrete evidence, was 'sheer moonshine, dear boy'.

There is often an air of romance about the word and its derivatives, hence that most treacly of nouns: honeymoon. Claudius and Gertrude are having an extended one of these in *Hamlet*, but the darkly-clad son is disenchanted, and separates their apiary sweetness from the harshness of the lunar light: he accuses the pair of them of 'honeying over the filthy sty'. His mother may be moonstruck with Claudius's charms, but the phrase that characterises Hamlet's attitude to this new and unwelcome stepfather of his would need to be borrowed from Malcolm Lowry: *lunar caustic*. This might be the eerie light of Walpurgisnacht, or even the Nuremburg Rallies. It is not that light which allows shadows to soften facial features, features which might be seen in all their brute materiality by the unforgiving daylight of the following morning. Sylvia Plath talks of the candle and the moon as 'those liars'. Gilbert and Sullivan are somewhat more brutal: speaking of his own daughter the rich attorney says: 'She may very well pass for forty-three/In the dusk with a light behind her'. We are entitled to assume that the backlight thus flattering the woman in question is lunar. This is presumably that effect which studio photographers call 'creative lighting'.

The scientific discoveries of the seventeenth century, starting with Galileo, presented us with a moon that was covered with pockmarks and asperities. So that was the end of any Aristotelian

"Mooning constitutes a type of revelation"

notion of the perfection of the heavens. Then the moonlanding in 1971 gave us a new sort of creature: a moonman. Yet the word here had preceded the landings by four centuries. In the sixteenth century a moonman was a gypsy, or sometimes a madman.

And there is, as always, the inevitable demotic demotion. *Mooning* constitutes a type of revelation, the nomenclature arising from the similarity in shape of the human rear end to the lunar body when in its fuller phases. Less revealing than flashing, which requires the removal of all accoutrements except – optionally – shoes and headgear, mooning is frequently preferred, as a partial exposition of the human anatomy through the window of a moving vehicle, often at speed. For which reason, it is more likely to occur on a midsummer night than in midwinter. And observers might occasionally wonder if they are dreaming. A moon, in any case, had from the middle of the eighteenth century signified the buttocks. And for those unlucky in their mooning, a moon from the early nineteenth century was also a month's imprisonment. To moontan is to engage in al fresco sexual activities during the nocturnal hours. This might be advised against by a moonshi, a wise man who – like so many of that rare species – came from the east, the word being derived from the Hindi word *munshi*, a writer or sometimes a secretary; one who knows how to keep a secret.

A moon-curser was one of the many dishonest link-boys who provided travellers in earlier centuries with a light through London, particularly around Lincoln's Inn Fields. They offered to light you through shadowy danger for pay, but just as often then robbed you. Those whose work is done by night accrue unwholesome reputations. A moonlighter, like a moonraker, is a thief, burglar or smuggler, and sometimes a prostitute, while the moonlight flit permits a shift in domicile under cover of darkness, leaving all the bills for the old place unpaid. One who behaves in this manner may sometimes be called a moon-shooter.

While Michael Jackson was still with us, he delighted the crowds with his moon walk, which mimicked the effects of trying to get about in unfamiliar gravitational conditions. But, as Shakespeare put it in one of his sonnets, 'The mortal moon hath her eclipse endured' and he has now departed this sublunar realm.

Odd that one of the most egregious uses of the word in the modern world appears to be an accident of transliteration. The Moonies do not get that way from gazing at the moonface, nor from their absorption in moonshine, but from their wholehearted commitment to the person and beliefs of the Reverend Sun Moon, a Korean, whose name in English appears to indicate that one might as well place one's bet both ways, but the original Korean means something like 'the word made clear'. He adjusted his name after he converted to Christianity, then formed the Holy Spirit Association for the Unification of World Christianity, aka the Unification Church. He organizes mass weddings for relative strangers in sports stadiums, all in the name of Jesus, whose millennial re-embodiment he claims to be. And he does not speak a word of English. The parents of the betrothed often conclude that their offspring are undoubtedly moonstruck.

The Lunar Society met once a month, as close to the full moon as possible to facilitate easier homeward travel at the end of the evening. Those distinguished scientific gentlemen might have been surprised to discover that our technological progress would mean that we go almost nowhere by the light of the full moon any more, unless we are up to some graveyard skulduggery. Light pollution has effectively quenched the moonlight in most modern cities.

FICTION

THE GLAZED MAQUETTE

Christine Shaw

I t was the evening of our sculpture class. Harriet was on her way to pick me up. Before she left I spoke to her on the telephone and asked her to drive carefully. The roads were icy and treacherous. I reminded her about the black ice at the bottom of the lane. 'Mother, don't go on,' I heard her say, 'my car can cope with any weather, didn't you know?' How would I know? I don't know anything about cars. What I do know is that she drives ferociously fast and is a constant worry to me.

At six-thirty, I gathered my things: handbag, scarf and gloves, and glanced at my watch. I paused for a moment then switched off the lights, feeling a warm glow inside. I slid my hand down the inside of the sofa behind the velvety cushions and pulled out an embroidered pouch. Inside was a pair of old opera glasses made from brass and mother-of-pearl. Discreetly, I peeked through the curtain and looked outside. Everything seemed perfectly still, perfectly silent.

Feeling safe and unseen, I peered through the eyepiece and panned across the darkness into the brightly-lit interior of the house opposite. The woman who lived there paced up and down with a baby harnessed to her chest. She was slender, in her thirties, and had sleek dark hair and a wide expressive face. She was dressed in a green tunic and pearl-grey stole. The baby was crying. I could see its crumpled face glowing, its small body straining beneath pink pyjamas. Distractedly, she glanced at her watch as she jiggled the baby back-and-forth. Her husband was opening drawers and pulling things out, not bothering to put anything back. He moved quickly, from drawer to drawer. It seemed he could not find what he was looking for and I could feel the tension mounting.

'What are you doing?' Giles asked. He was standing behind me in the darkness.

I turned from the window startled, my heart thumping, 'Giles! You scared me,' I said, staring at the outline of his body, adjusting my eyes to the shadowy light.

'I thought as much. You were spying on them again weren't you?' he said.

'I was looking for Harriet,' I said. 'Can't I look out anymore without having to explain myself?'

'Why the binoculars?'

'Giles stop! –'

'You promised me, Eleanor!'

I could hear the wheezing deep inside his chest. I wanted him to go back to bed. 'I was only –'

'You were only what?'

I paused for a moment. 'Why are you so angry?'

He didn't answer. Giles hates it when I respond to a question with a question. He stepped back and switched on the light. 'Look, I insist that you stop this at once. I can understand your curiosity to a point, but this spying of yours is getting out of hand.'

Squinting now under the bright light, I turned to him. 'I'm not a voyeur, so stop treating me like one.' But of course, I had told a lie and we both knew it. I heard the baby crying inside my head, incessant and demanding. I knew the rage that arose inside every parent whose baby cried incessantly. At times, you wanted to shake it until it stopped – you wanted to shake it because you could not bear it any longer, because the crying was threatening your sanity. Surely, every parent who has a child knows this, but how many lose control?

Giles sat down on the sofa and leant forward with his elbows resting on his knees. The fine, silvery hair across the top of his head was thinning, revealing a smooth scalp.

'You must not provoke him in any way; he's irascible.'

'They need support, Giles,' I said, 'if only they'd ask me to baby-sit then they could both go out and –'

'We've been through this before,' he said, glaring at me. 'I forbid you to go anywhere near them, is that clear?'

Giles had witnessed an incident the other evening and was not prepared to forgive. It was pointless arguing with him – my husband is stubborn and set in his ways but it didn't stop me yearning to have a child in my life again.

'Giles, why don't you go back to bed, you look dreadful?'

'I feel dreadful,' he said, 'I came down for some medicine, the bottle upstairs is empty. Do we have any more?'

'I'll have a look,' I said, dutifully.

'I suspect you're still going then?' I heard him say. 'It doesn't matter how ill I am, you'll still go, won't you?'

'You know I won't be gone long,' I said, walking towards him.

'Do you have to go? The weather is dreadful this evening.'

I didn't answer. I found the bottle and poured the thick pink syrup into a plastic dispenser and spooned it into his mouth. I was determined not to miss the class and followed him back into the hall and watched him slowly mount the stairs. When I heard the bedsprings creak, I switched off the light and went back to the window, to the opera glasses.

The brightly-lit room across the road reminded me of a stage-set. How strange and yet familiar it felt to be watching from such close quarters. In the mirror, she adjusted her stole and smoothed her hair. To her right was a painting—a blur of yellows and blues, possibly a seascape or an abstract, I wasn't sure. The woman was leaning over now searching behind cushions. She picked up her handbag and looked inside. Behind her, I could see a glass cabinet, partly out of view. It contained porcelain figurines: ballerinas, flower girls and reclining nudes, each one on a revolving glass carousel that sparkled with light from within. I watched it circle round and round, entranced by the delicate silent forms, moulded to perfection.

Standing now behind the cold glass, she pointed a finger at him accusingly. I could see her mouth working, her face animated. It was like a scene from a kitchen-sink drama. He put the baby down and offered up the palms of his hands in a defiant, 'stop-immediately' gesture. Guiltily, I pulled the curtain closer and held my breath as he lunged forward and grabbed her by the throat and shook her. I put the glasses down and glanced at my watch through a chink in the curtains, my whole body trembling. It was approaching seven. I felt my way through the darkness to the front door.

Outside, the air was freezing. My breath escaped in delicate plumes as I gingerly made my way down the garden path. At the gate I noticed a flare of headlights approaching. It was Harriet's car. Harriet had milky skin and red hair that was thick and ungovernable. She pulled up alongside the kerb, reached across and pushed open the door, 'Hi Mum, sorry I'm late,' she said, as I climbed in. Inside the car it was warm and cosy and smelt of leather and newness.

'Have you been waiting long? You look cold.'

'No, no, I'm fine,' I said, fastening my seat belt.

'I can smell the cold on you. How long have you been standing there?'

'Not long. I'm okay Harriet, really. How are you?'

'Okay' she said, as we drove off. 'What did you mean on the phone, when you said 'don't pip your horn'?'

I paused for a moment before answering.

'Well?'

'It's the man opposite. I don't think he's well.'

'What's wrong with him?'

'I don't know –'

'It was Dad, wasn't it?' she said, as we drove on. 'You wouldn't ring me at work for something so trivial – I bet he put you up to it, didn't he?'

I didn't answer. I glanced at a row of smart shops lit up against the night, feeling the force of the car as it accelerated away.

Harriet has not spoken to her father for months. She thinks he is a hypochondriac. She thinks he uses his ailments as a way of controlling me. I listen to my daughter but I think she's too hard on him.

The air inside the workshop was heavy with aerosol fumes, resins and paint. I walked over to the storeroom. The walls were furnished with shelves containing tools of every kind. Above the tools were plaster casts, bits of mesh and wire, tins of acrylic paint and hefty bags full of white powder and clay, and on the far wall was a cupboard containing sieves, rolling pins, chamois leathers and natural sponges. A young woman holding a piece of cheesewire cut me a chunk from the slab of clay wrapped in polythene.

Back at the bench I took the moist clay in my hands. It felt cool and responsive as though it was alive and breathing. I still couldn't decide what to make – a figure perhaps? Everyone in the room was busy in their own private space working to their own creative impulses. Across the room Harriet worked on a large slab of granite. She wore safety goggles as she chipped away at the grey stone, the muscles in her arms taut, her face full of concentration. Harriet's sculptures were invariably hewn out of solid rock. She liked to test and reinvent, she liked to take risks. For me stone is too unforgiving, I prefer clay. With clay you have safety nets, you know where you're at – you can build solid structures and smooth over cracks, it's malleable and adaptable.

As I began to knead and wedge the clay on a board, my mind ran back to my neighbours. I didn't even know their names or what they did for a living, but I felt as though I knew them. I divided the clay into three pieces, took a piece of copper wire twisted it into shape, covered the wire with clay and worked outwards from the core. As it began to take shape I carved the features with a paring knife, making several grooves in the clay between the figures. With the remainder I stretched the pieces and rolled them into coils. I added more clay bit-by-bit, smoothed it down and wet it to keep it moist. At the end of the evening I wrapped the maquette in polythene and stored it away. Harriet was waiting for me by the door her face dark and brooding.

'Are you okay?'

'No,' she said, emphatically, 'Jordan can't make *Twelfth Night* on Friday.'

'Did he phone you?' I asked, as we walked down the corridor.

'No, he sent me a text message.'

'I'm sorry, Harriet. Can't you get a refund?'

She shook her head. 'The theatre doesn't give refunds.'

On the way home the road was blocked. Vehicles were turning around to avoid the jam. On the other side of the road, a gritter thundered past with its amber lights flashing, spraying grit across the road. I felt it rain down on Harriet's car and heard her curse. I was temporarily lost in my own thoughts, thinking about my evening's work, trying to picture how it would look when it was fired and glazed. The three figures were linked together, forming a circle. Their hands were threaded as a way of symbolising love and harmony. I was pleased with my progress and started to think about making a larger model when Harriet blasted her horn at the driver in front. We were gridlocked. The police had arrived and were directing traffic. Giles flashed through my mind. I wondered whether I ought to phone him to tell him that I'd be late, but I pictured him asleep and angry at being woken up. Harriet tapped her hand on the steering wheel impatiently, then reached into her handbag, pulled out an envelope and slapped it down on the dashboard.

'There, two theatre tickets! Will you come with me?'

I paused before answering. 'I'd like to join you, but what about your father? You know how he hates being left alone.'

'Will you stop worrying about him. He'll cope for one evening, you know he will. Besides, you haven't been to the theatre for years.'

I knew I couldn't accept her offer. Giles would make too much fuss. 'Harriet, its better that you ask somebody else, you know how it is.'

'Well I think you're a fool,' she said, as she inched the car forward. The cars in front were gradually beginning to move. 'Why can't you assert yourself for once? Tell him!'

I looked at her but didn't answer. I knew that somewhere inside Giles and Harriet loved each other. If only Harriet could see past his weaknesses.

As we drove over the humpback-bridge onto the lane, I reminded Harriet about the black ice, how treacherous it was at the bottom. I felt a sense of relief when we pulled up outside the house until I noticed the lights were on. Giles was up, he would be furious because I hadn't phoned. I was reaching for my handbag when a truck on the other side of the lane skidded and swerved across narrowly missing us. Instinctively, Harriet blasted her horn.

'Stop!' I heard myself shout, grabbing her forearm. 'Harriet, you shouldn't have done that.'

'He nearly hit us! He nearly rammed into my car, what do you expect?'

I was thinking about the baby when I glanced across at the neighbour's house. He was stood inside the window looking out. Seconds later he threw back the door and came down the path towards us.

Automatically, I flicked down the car's central locking switch, my heart beating frantically.

'Do you know what time it is?' he shouted, his face close to the window on Harriet's side.

Harriet glanced at the clock on the dashboard and lowering the window spoke to him, 'Yes, I am aware of the time. What about it?'

'I'm sorry,' I interrupted. 'My daughter didn't mean to sound her horn so aggressively – it's just that a lorry –'

'I don't want to hear your excuses,' he said furious, his cold breath seeping into the car. 'You've woken up my baby, and you have no idea how long it took me to get her to sleep.'

On seeing her father approach in his dressing gown, Harriet closed the window and immediately got out. I didn't have the courage to follow her. I closed my eyes and willed myself to think of something pleasant. I would paint the maquette, I thought, and glaze it, and present it to the neighbours when things were back to normal. They collected figurines, lots of them. I pictured the glass carousel, bright and magical, and endlessly revolving. I knew they would accept my gift. It would be a peace offering, a symbol of friendship and a start of something new.

CONTRIBUTORS

Alison Brackenbury's eighth collection is due from Carcanet in April 2013. New poems can be seen at her website: www.alisonbrackenbury.co.uk.

Casi Dylan is Training Manager for The Reader Organisation.

Grace Farrington is a PhD student at the University of Liverpool. Her research, based on a year spent as a GIR project worker in Mersey Care NHS Trust, explores the use of literature in relation to health and wellbeing.

Pat Farrington was a director in BBC Schools Television where she started writing song lyrics for children. After leaving, she began to write poetry for adults and has now had more than a dozen poems published in magazines such as *Orbis*, *South* and *Decanto*.

Patrick Fisher is a project worker with young people, working for The Reader Organisation in Glasgow.

Joseph Gold was born in London. He is a pioneer in the field of human-scale personal reading of literature. Books include the inspirational *Read for Your Life: Literature as a Life Support System* and *The Story Species: Our Life-Literature Connection*. He lives in Northern Ontario.

Rebecca Goss's first full-length collection *The Anatomy of Structures*, was published by Flambard Press in 2010. She was Highly Commended in The Forward Prize in 2010. 'Her Birth' is taken from her next collection, about the death of her daughter Ella, aged sixteen months, in 2008.

John Kinsella's most recent book is *Activist Poetics: Anarchy in the Avon Valley* (Liverpool University Press, 2010). His latest poetry volume is, *Armour* (Picador) November 2011. He is a Fellow of Churchill College, Cambridge, and a Professorial Research Fellow at University of Western Australia.

John Levett has published four collections, won the National Poetry Competition and been shortlisted for the Whitbread Poetry Award. *A Short History of Mornings* appeared from Shoestring Press in 2010.

Roy McFarlane was born in Birmingham of Jamaican parentage. His poems have appeared in anthologies including *Out of Bounds* (Bloodaxe 2012) and *Celebrate Wha* (Smokestaks 2011) which he co-edited. He was Birmingham Poet Laureate in 2010/2011.

Ian McMillan was born in 1956 and has been a freelance writer/performer /broadcaster since 1981. He presents *The Verb* on BBC Radio 3 every Friday night.

Julie-ann Rowell's pamphlet, *Convergence*, was a Poetry Book Society choice. Her first collection, *Letters North*, was shortlisted for the Inaugural Michael Murphy Memorial Prize, 2011, for best first collection in Britain and Ireland. She teaches poetry classes in Bristol.

Christine Shaw has completed an MA in English Literature at The University of Manchester and is now pursuing a range of creative interests: writing short stories, working on a novel, and making a range of one of a kind rag dolls.

Janet Suzman was born in S.A, pursued her love of English in general and Shakespeare in particular by coming to Britain, with frequent forays into other engrossing dramatic landscapes in Russia, or Norway, or the Attic plain. Occasional directing keeps the wolf from the door. *Not Hamlet* (Oberon Books) is her latest book.

Raymond Tallis is a philosopher, poet, novelist and cultural critic. His most recent book is *In Defence of Wonder and other Philosophical Reflections* (Acumen 2012).

Alan Wall is a novelist, short story writer, poet and essayist. His latest novel *Badmouth* will appear soon from Quartet Books. He is professor of Writing and Literature at the University of Chester.

Margaret Wickham was born in Germany. 90 next year, she was one of the first women to get a full degree from Oxford. At 27 she was a pioneering teacher of girls in Anglo-Egyptian Sudan; later headmistress of St George's School, Ascot. After a stroke she entered Croft House Nursing and Residential Home, where she has lived for the last nine years.

Distribution Information

Trade orders Contact Mark Chilver, Magazine Department, Central Books

    email: mark@centralbooks.com
    web: www.centralbooks.com
    tel: 0845 458 9925   fax: 0845 458 9912
    Central Books, 99 Wallis Road, London, E9 5LN

All other queries regarding trade orders or institutional subscriptions
Contact The Reader Office

    email: magazine@thereader.org.uk
    tel: 0151 207 7207

SUBSCRIBE

Just £18 per year with Direct Debit

Either print off an order form from our website (www.
thereader.org.uk), call us on 0151 207 7207 or email
(magazine@thereader.org.uk) and we will send you a form
in the post.

Cost by Cheque or PayPal:

UK	4 issues	£24.00	(including p&p)
Abroad	4 issues	£36.00	(including p&p)

Please make cheques payable to The Reader Organisation
and post to: The Reader Organisation, FREEPOST RSSL-
UHCB-EKKE, The Friary Centre, Bute Street, Liverpool,
L5 3LA.

Don't forget to include your name and address, and the
issue number with which you would like your subscription to begin.

Overseas readers: your cheapest method is by PayPal via
our website: www.thereader.org.uk.

Please direct email enquiries to:
subscriptions@thereader.org.uk

See p.11 for our Christmas Gift Subscription offer

the reader